Vol. VI

THE MATTERHORN

SEEING EUROPE
WITH FAMOUS AUTHORS

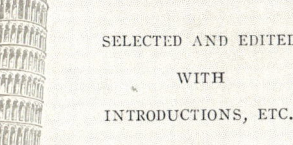
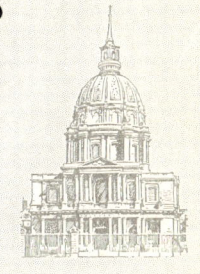

SELECTED AND EDITED

WITH

INTRODUCTIONS, ETC.

BY

FRANCIS W. HALSEY

*Editor of "Great Epochs in American History"
Associate Editor of "The World's Famous Orations"
and of "The Best of the World's Classics," etc.*

IN TEN

VOLUMES

ILLUSTRATED

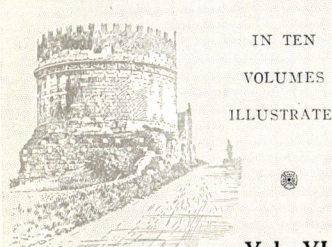

**Vol. VI
GERMANY, AUSTRIA-HUNGARY,
AND SWITZERLAND
Part Two**

FUNK & WAGNALLS COMPANY

NEW YORK AND LONDON

Copyright, 1914, by
FUNK & WAGNALLS COMPANY
[*Printed in the United States of America*]

VI

CONTENTS OF VOLUME VI

Germany, Austria-Hungary, and Switzerland—Part Two

VI. HUNGARY—*(Continued)*

	PAGE
HUNGARIAN BATHS AND RESORTS—By H. Tornai de Kövér	1
THE GIPSIES—By H. Tornai de Kövér	5

VII. AUSTRIA'S ADRIATIC PORTS

TRIESTE AND POLA—By Edward A. Freeman	9
SPALATO—By Edward A. Freeman	18
RAGUSA—By Harry De Windt	25
CATTARO—By Edward A. Freeman	29

VIII. OTHER AUSTRIAN SCENES

CRACOW—By Mènie Muriel Dowie	34
ON THE ROAD TO PRAGUE—By Bayard Taylor	40
THE CAVE OF ADELSBERG—By George Stillman Hillard	46
THE MONASTERY OF MÖLK—By Thomas Frognall Dibdin	50

CONTENTS

	PAGE
THROUGH THE TYROL—By William Cullen Bryant	53
IN THE DOLOMITES—By Archibald Campbell Knowles	61
CORTINA—By Amelia B. Edwards	67

IX. ALPINE RESORTS

THE CALL OF THE MOUNTAINS—By Frederick Harrison	71
INTERLAKEN AND THE JUNGFRAU—By Archibald Campbell Knowles	74
THE ALTDORF OF WILLIAM TELL—By W. D. M'Crackan	80
LUCERNE—By Victor Tissot	83
ZURICH—By W. D. M'Crackan	87
THE RIGI—By W. D. M'Crackan	92
CHAMOUNI—AN AVALANCHE—By Percy Bysshe Shelley	94
ZERMATT—By Archibald Campbell Knowles	96
PONTRESINA AND ST. MORITZ—By Victor Tissot	101
GENEVA—By Francis H. Gribble	105
THE CASTLE OF CHILLON—By Harriet Beecher Stowe	109
BY RAIL UP THE GORNER-GRAT—By Archibald Campbell Knowles	113

CONTENTS

	PAGE
THROUGH THE ST. GOTHARD INTO ITALY—By Victor Tissot	116

X. ALPINE MOUNTAIN CLIMBING

FIRST ATTEMPTS HALF A CENTURY AGO—By Edward Whymper	119
FIRST TO THE TOP OF THE MATTERHORN—By Edward Whymper	127
THE LORD FRANCIS DOUGLAS TRAGEDY—By Edward Whymper	133
AN ASCENT OF MONTE ROSA (1858)—By John Tyndall	139
MONT BLANC ASCENDED, HUXLEY GOING PART WAY—By John Tyndall	148
THE JUNGFRAU-JOCH—By Sir Leslie Stephen	165

XI. OTHER ALPINE TOPICS

THE GREAT ST. BERNARD HOSPICE—By Archibald Campbell Knowles	171
AVALANCHES—By Victor Tissot	174
HUNTING THE CHAMOIS—By Victor Tissot	178
THE CELEBRITIES OF GENEVA—By Francis H. Gribble	181

LIST OF ILLUSTRATIONS

VOLUME VI

FRONTISPIECE

    THE MATTERHORN

PRECEDING PAGE 1

    KURSAAL AT MARIENBAD
    MARIENBAD, AUSTRIA
    MONASTERY OF ST. ULRIC AND AFRA, AUGSBURG
    MONASTERY OF MÖLK ON THE DANUBE ABOVE VIENNA
    MEMORIAL TABLET AND ROAD IN THE IRON GATE OF THE DANUBE
    QUAY AT FIUME
    ROYAL PALACE IN BUDAPEST
    HOUSES OF PARLIAMENT, BUDAPEST
    SUSPENSION BRIDGE OVER THE DANUBE AT BUDAPEST
    STREET IN BUDAPEST
    CATHEDRAL OF SPALATO
    REGUSA, DALMATIA
    MIRAMAR
    GENEVA
    REGATTA DAY ON LAKE GENEVA
    VITZNAU, THE LAKE TERMINUS OF THE RIGI RAILROAD
    RHINE FALLS NEAR SCHAFFHAUSEN

LIST OF ILLUSTRATIONS

FOLLOWING PAGE 96

    PONTRESINA IN THE ENGADINE
    ST. MORITZ IN THE ENGADINE
    FRIBOURG
    BERNE
    VIVEY, LAKE GENEVA
    THE TURNHALLE, ZURICH
    INTERLAKEN
    LUCERNE
    VIADUCTS ON AN ALPINE RAILWAY
    THE WOLFORT VIADUCT
    BALMAT—SAUSSURE MONUMENT IN CHAMONIX
    ROOFED WOODEN BRIDGE AT LUCERNE
    THE CASTLE OF CHILLON
    CLOUD EFFECT ABOVE INTERLAKEN
    DAVOS IN WINTER

THE KURSAL AT MARIENBAD

MARIENBAD, AUSTRIA

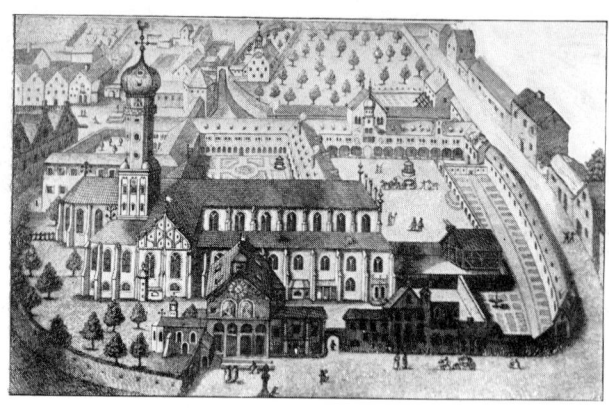

THE MONASTERY OF ST. ULRIC AND AFRA, AT AUGSBURG IN BAVARIA

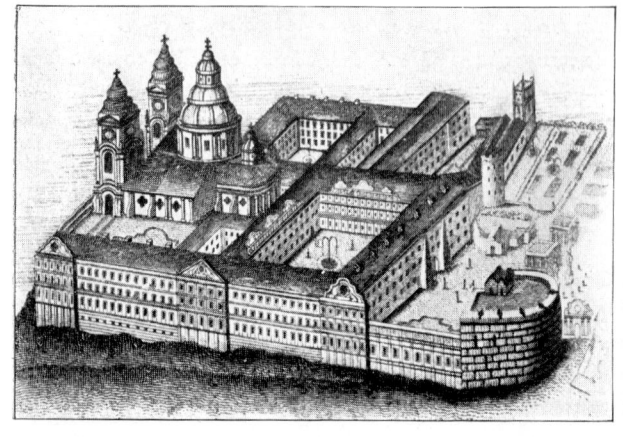

THE MONASTERY OF MÖLK ON THE DANUBE ABOVE VIENNA

Courtesy Brentano's

MEMORIAL TABLET AND ROAD IN THE IRON GATE
OF THE DANUBE

Courtesy Brentano's

THE QUAY OF FIUME AT THE HEAD OF THE ADRIATIC

Courtesy Brentano's

THE ROYAL PALACE AT BUDAPEST

Courtesy Brentano's

THE HOUSES OF PARLIAMENT AT BUDAPEST

Courtesy Brentano's

THE SUSPENSION BRIDGE OVER THE DANUBE AT BUDAPEST

Courtesy Brentano's

STREET IN BUDAPEST

THE CATHEDRAL OF SPALATO
Burial-place of the Emperor Diocletian

RAGUSA, DALMATIA

MIRAMAR
Long the home of the ex-Empress Carlotta of Mexico

GENEVA

Courtesy Swiss Federal Railway

REGATTA DAY ON LAKE GENEVA

Courtesy Swiss Federal Railway

VITZNAU, THE LAKE TERMINUS OF THE RIGI RAILROAD

THE RHINE FALLS NEAR SCHAFFHAUSEN

VI

HUNGARY
(Continued)

HUNGARIAN BATHS AND RESORTS*

BY H. TORNAI DE KÖVËR

In Hungary there are great quantities of unearthed riches, and not only in the form of gold. These riches are the mineral waters that abound in the country and have been the natural medicine of the people for many years. Water in itself was always worshiped by the Hungarians in the earliest ages, and they have found out through experience for which ailment the different waters may be used. There are numbers of small watering-places in the most primitive state, which are visited by the peasants from far and wide, more especially those that are good for rheumatism.

Like all people that work much in the open, the Hungarian in old age feels the aching of his limbs. The Carpathians are full of such baths, some of them quite primitive; others are used more as summer resorts, where the well-to-do town people build their villas; others, again, like Tátra Füred, Tátra Lomnicz, Csorba, and many others, have every accommodation and are visited by people from all over Europe.

*From "Hungary." Published by the Macmillan Co.

SEEING EUROPE WITH FAMOUS AUTHORS

In former times Germans and Poles were the chief visitors, but now people come from all parts to look at the wonderful ice-caves (where one can skate in the hottest summer), the waterfalls, and the great pine forests, and make walking, driving, and riding tours right up to the snow-capped mountains, preferring the comparative quiet of this Alpine district to that of Switzerland. Almost every place has some special mineral water, and among the greatest wonders of Hungary are the hot mud-baths of Pöstyén.

This place is situated at the foot of the lesser Carpathians, and is easily reached from the main line of the railway. The scenery is lovely and the air healthy, but this is nothing compared to the wondrous waters and hot mire which oozes out of the earth in the vicinity of the river Vág. Hot sulfuric water, which contains radium, bubbles up in all parts of Pöstyén, and even the bed of the cold river is full of steaming hot mud. As far back as 1551 we know of the existence of Pöstyén as a natural cure, and Sir Spencer Wells, the great English doctor, wrote about these waters in 1888. They are chiefly good for rheumatism, gout, neuralgia, the strengthening of broken bones, strains, and also for scrofula.

On the premises there is a quaint museum with crutches and all sort of sticks and invalid chairs left there by their former owners in grateful acknowledgment of the wonderful waters and mire that had healed them. Of late there has been much comfort added; great new baths have been built, villas and new

HUNGARY

hotels added, so that there is accommodation for rich and poor alike. The natural heat of the mire is 140 degrees Fahrenheit. Plenty of amusements are supplied for those who are not great sufferers—tennis, shooting, fishing, boating, and swimming being all obtainable. The bathing-place and all the adjoining land belongs to Count Erdödy.

Another place of the greatest importance is the little bath "Parád," hardly three hours from Budapest, situated in the heart of the mountains of the "Mátra." It is the private property of Count Károlyi. The place is primitive and has not even electric light. Its waters are a wonderful combination of iron and alkaline, but this is not the most important feature. Besides the baths there is a strong spring of arsenic water which, through a fortunate combination, is stronger and more digestible than Roncegno and all the other first-rate waters of that kind in the world.

Not only in northern Hungary does one find wondrous cures, it is the same in Transylvania. There are healing and splendid mineral waters for common use all over the country lying idle and awaiting the days when its owners will be possest by the spirit of enterprise. Borszek, Szováta, and many others are all wonders in their way, waters that would bring in millions to their owners if only worked properly. Szováta, boasts of a lake containing such an enormous proportion of salt that not even the human body can sink into its depths.

In the south there is Herkulesfürdö, renowned

as much for the beauty of its scenery as for its waters. Besides those mentioned there are all the summer pleasure resorts; the best of these are situated along Lake Balaton. The tepid water, long sandbanks, and splendid air from the forests make them specially healthy for delicate children. But not only have the bathing-places beautiful scenery from north to south and from east to west, in general the country abounds in Alpine districts, waterfalls, caves, and other wonders of nature. The most beautiful tour is along the river Vág, starting from the most northerly point in Hungary near the beautiful old stronghold of Árva in the county of Árva.

All those that care to see a country as it really is, and do not mind going out of the usual beaten track of the globe-trotter, should go down the river Vág. It can not be done by steamer, or any other comfortable contrivance, one must do it on a raft, as the rapids of the river are not to be passed by any other means. The wood is transported in this way from the mountain regions to the south, and for two days one passes through the most beautiful scenery. Fantastic castles loom at the top of mountain peaks, and to each castle is attached a page of the history of the Middle Ages, when the great noblemen were also the greatest robbers of the land, and the people were miserable serfs, who did all the work and were taxed and robbed by their masters. Castles, wild mountain districts, rugged passes, villages, and ruins are passed like a beautiful panorama. The river rushes along, foaming and dashing over sharp rocks. The people are reliable and very clever in handling the raft, which requires great skill, especially when conducted over the falls at low water. Sometimes there is only one little spot where the raft can pass, and to conduct it over those rapids requires absolute knowledge of every rock hidden under the shallow falls. If notice is given in time, a rude hut will be built on the raft to give shelter and make it possible to have meals cooked, altho in the simplest way (consisting of baked potatoes and stew), by the Slavs who are in charge of the raft. If anything better is wanted it must be ordered by stopping at the larger towns; but to have it done in the simple way is entering into the true spirit of the voyage.

THE GIPSIES*

BY H. TORNAI DE KÖVËR

Gipsies! Music! Dancing! These are words of magic to the rich and poor, noblemen and peasant alike, if he be a true Hungarian. There are two kinds of gipsies. The wandering thief, who can not be made to take up any occupation. These are a terribly lawless and immoral people, and there seems to be no way of altering their life and habits, altho much has been written on the subject to improve matters; but the Government has shown itself to be helpless as yet. These people live here and there, in fact everywhere, leading a

*From "Hungary." Published by the Macmillan Co.

wandering life in carts, and camp wherever night overtakes them. After some special evil-doing they will wander into Rumania or Russia and come back after some years when the deed of crime has been forgotten. Their movements are so quick and silent that they outwit the best detectives of the police force. They speak the gipsy language, but often a half-dozen other languages besides, in their peculiar chanting voice. Their only occupation is stealing, drinking, smoking, and being a nuisance to the country in every way.

The other sort of gipsies consist of those that have squatted down in the villages some hundreds of years ago. They live in a separate part of the village, usually at the end, are dirty and untidy and even an unruly people, but for the most part have taken up some honest occupation. They make the rough, unbaked earth bricks that the peasant cottages are mostly made of, are tinkers and blacksmiths, but they do the lowest kind of work too. Besides these, however, there are the talented ones. The musical gipsy begins to handle his fiddle as soon as he can toddle. The Hungarians brought their love of music with them from Asia. Old parchments have been found which denote that they had their songs and war-chants at the time of the "home-making," and church and folk-songs from their earliest Christian period. Peasant and nobleman are musical alike—it runs in the race. The gipsies that have settled among them caught up the love of music and are now the best interpreters of the Hungarian songs.

HUNGARY

The people have got so used to their "blackies," as they call them, that no lesser or greater fête day can pass without the gipsy band having ample work to do in the form of playing for the people. Their instruments are the fiddle, 'cello, viola, clarinet, tárogato (a Hungarian specialty), and, above all, the cymbal. The tárogato looks like a grand piano with the top off. It stands on four legs like a table and has wires drawn across it; on these wires the player performs with two little sticks, that are padded at the ends with cotton-wool. The sound is wild and weird, but if well played very beautiful indeed. The gipsies seldom compose music. The songs come into life mostly on the spur of the moment. In the olden days war-songs and long ballads were the most usual form of music. The seventeenth and eighteenth centuries were specially rich in the production of songs that live even now. At that time the greatest gipsy musician was a woman: her name was "Czinka Panna," and she was called the Gipsy Queen. With the change of times the songs are altered too, and now they are mostly lyric. Csárdás is the quick form of music, and tho of different melodies it must always be kept to the same rhythm. This is not much sung to, but is the music for the national dance. The peasants play on a little wooden flute which is called the "Tilinko," or "Furulya," and they know hundreds of sad folk-songs and lively Csárdás. While living their isolated lives in the great plains they compose many a beautiful song.

It is generally from the peasants and the

musical country gentry that the gipsy gets his music. He learns the songs after a single hearing, and plays them exactly according to the singer's wish. The Hungarian noble when singing with the gipsies is capable of giving the dark-faced boys every penny he has. In this manner many a young nobleman has been ruined, and the gipsies make nothing of it, because they are just like their masters and "spend easily earned money easily," as the saying goes. Where there is much music there is much dancing. Every Sunday afternoon after church the villages are lively with the sound of the gipsy band, and the young peasant boys and girls dance.

The Slovaks of the north play a kind of bagpipe, which reminds one of the Scotch ones; but the songs of the Slovak have got very much mixed with the Hungarian. The Rumanian music is of a distinct type, but the dances all resemble the Csárdás, with the difference that the quick figures in the Slav and Rumanian dances are much more grotesque and verging on acrobatism.

VII

AUSTRIA'S ADRIATIC PORTS

TRIESTE AND POLA*

BY EDWARD A. FREEMAN

Trieste stands forth as a rival of Venice, which has, in a low practical view of things, outstript her. Italian zeal naturally cries for the recovery of a great city, once part of the old Italian kingdom, and whose speech is largely, perhaps chiefly, Italian to this day. But, a cry of "Italia Irredenta," however far it may go, must not go so far as this. Trieste, a cosmopolitan city on a Slavonic shore, can not be called Italian in the same sense as the lands and towns so near Verona which yearn to be as Verona is. Let Trieste be the rival, even the eyesore, of Venice, still Southern Germany must have a mouth.

We might, indeed, be better pleased to see Trieste a free city, the southern fellow of Lübeck, Bremen and Hamburg; but it must not be forgotten that the Archduke of Austria and Lord of Trieste reigns at Trieste by a far better right than that by which he reigns at Cattaro and Spizza. The present people of

*From "Sketches from the Subject and Neighbour Lands of Venice." Published by the Macmillan Co.

SEEING EUROPE WITH FAMOUS AUTHORS

Trieste did not choose him, but the people of Trieste five hundred years back did choose the forefather of his great-grandmother. Compared with the grounds of which kingdoms, duchies, counties, and lordships, are commonly held in that neighborhood, such a claim as this must be allowed to be respectable indeed.

The great haven of Trieste may almost at pleasure be quoted as either confirming or contradicting the rule that it is not in the great commercial cities of Europe that we are to look for the choicest or the most plentiful remains of antiquity. Sometimes the cities themselves are of modern foundation; in other cases the cities themselves, as habitations of men and seats of commerce, are of the hoariest antiquity, but the remains of their early days have perished through their very prosperity. Massalia,* with her long history, with her double wreath of freedom, the city which withstood Cæsar and which withstood Charles of Anjou, is bare of monuments of her early days. She has been the victim of her abiding good fortune. We can look down from the height on the Phôkaian harbor; but for actual memorials of the men who fled from the Persian, of the men who defied the Roman and the Angevin, we might look as well at Liverpool or at Havre.

Genoa, Venice herself, are hardly real exceptions; they were indeed commercial cities, but they were ruling cities also, and, as ruling cities, they reared monuments which could hardly pass away. What are we to say to the

*The modern Marseilles.

AUSTRIA'S ADRIATIC PORTS

modern rival of Venice, the upstart rebel, one is tempted to say, against the supremacy of the Hadriatic Queen? Trieste, at the head of her gulf, with the hills looking down to her haven, with the snowy mountains which seem to guard the approach from the other side of her inland sea, with her harbor full of the ships of every nation, her streets echoing with every tongue, is she to be reckoned as an example of the rule or an exception to it?

No city at first sight seems more thoroughly modern; old town and new, wide streets and narrow, we search them in vain for any of those vestiges of past times which in some cities meet us at every step. Compare Trieste with Ancona;* we miss the arch of Trajan on the haven; we miss the cupola of Saint Cyriacus soaring in triumph above the triumphal monument of the heathen. We pass through the stately streets of the newer town, we thread the steep ascents which lead us to the older town above, and we nowhere light on any of those little scraps of ornamental architecture, a window, a doorway, a column, which meet us at every step in so many of the cities of Italy.

Yet the monumental wealth of Trieste is all but equal to the monumental wealth of Ancona. At Ancona we have the cathedral church and the triumphal arch; so we have at Trieste; tho at Trieste we have nothing to set against the grand front of the lower and

*An ancient Italian town on the Adriatic, founded by Syracusans about 300 B.C. and still an important seaport.

smaller church of Ancona. But at Ancona arch and duomo both stand out before all eyes; at Trieste both have to be looked for. The church of Saint Justus at Trieste crowns the hill as well as the church of Saint Cyriacus at Ancona; but it does not in the same way proclaim its presence. The castle, with its ugly modern fortifications, rises again above the church; and the duomo of Trieste, with its shapeless outline and its low, heavy, unsightly campanile, does not catch the eyes like the Greek cross and cupola of Ancona.

Again at Trieste the arch could never, in its best days, have been a rival to the arch at Ancona; and now either we have to hunt it out by an effort, or else it comes upon us suddenly, standing, as it does, at the head of a mean street on the ascent to the upper town. Of a truth it can not compete with Ancona or with Rimini, with Orange* or with Aosta. But the duomo, utterly unsightly as it is in a general view, puts on quite a new character when we first see the remains of pagan times imprisoned in the lower stage of the heavy campanile, still more so when we take our first glance of its wonderful interior. At the first glimpse we see that here there is a mystery to be unraveled; and as we gradually find the clue to the marvelous changes which it has undergone, we feel that outside show is not everything, and that, in point both of antiquity and of in-

*The city in Provence where have survived a beautiful Roman arch and a stupendous Roman theater in which classical plays are still given each year by actors from the Theatre Français.

terest, tho not of actual beauty, the double basilica of Trieste may claim no mean place among buildings of its own type. Even after the glories of Rome and Ravenna, the Tergestine church may be studied with no small pleasure and profit, as an example of a kind of transformation of which neither Rome nor Ravenna can supply another example. . . .

The other ancient relic at Trieste is the small triumphal arch. On one side it keeps its Corinthian pilasters; on the other they are imbedded in a house. The arch is in a certain sense double; but the two are close together, and touch in the keystone. The Roman date of this arch can not be doubted; but legends connect it both with Charles the Great and with Richard of Poitou and of England, a prince about whom Tergestine fancy has been very busy. The popular name of the arch is Arco Riccardo.

Such, beside some fragments in the museum, are all the remains that the antiquary will find in Trieste; not much in point of number, but, in the case of the duomo at least, of surpassing interest in their own way. But the true merit of Trieste is not in anything that it has itself, its church, its arch, its noble site. Placed there at the head of the gulf, on the borders of two great portions of the Empire, it leads to the land which produced that line of famous Illyrian Emperors who for a while checked the advance of our own race in the world's history, and it leads specially to the chosen home of the greatest among them.* The chief glory of

*Diocletian.

SEEING EUROPE WITH FAMOUS AUTHORS

Trieste, after all, is that it is the way to Spalato. . . .

At Pola the monuments of Pietas Julia claim the first place; the basilica, tho not without a certain special interest, comes long after them. The character of the place is fixt by the first sight of it; we see the present and we see the more distant past; the Austrian navy is to be seen, and the amphitheater is to be seen. But intermediate times have little to show; if the duomo strikes the eye at all, it strikes it only by the extreme ugliness of its outside, nor is there anything very taking, nothing like the picturesque castle of Pirano, in the works which occupy the site of the colonial capitol. The duomo should not be forgotten; even the church of Saint Francis is worth a glance; but it is in the remains of the Roman colony, in the amphitheater, the arches, the temples, the fragments preserved in that temple which serves, as at Nîmes,* for a museum, that the real antiquarian wealth of Pola lies. . . .

The known history of Pola begins with the Roman conquest of Istria in 178 B.C. The town became a Roman colony and a flourishing seat of commerce. Its action on the republican side in the civil war brought on it the vengeance of the second Cæsar. But the destroyer became the restorer, and Pietas Julia, in the height of its greatness, far surpassed the extent either of the elder or the younger Pola. Like all cities of this region, Pola kept up its importance down to the days of the Carlovingian

*A reference to the exquisite Maison Carrée of Nîmes.

AUSTRIA'S ADRIATIC PORTS

Empire, the specially flourishing time of the whole district being that of Gothic and Byzantine dominion at Ravenna. A barbarian king, the Roxolan Rasparasanus, is said to have withdrawn to Pola after the submission of his nation to Hadrian; and the panegyrists of the Flavian house rank Pola along with Trier and Autun among the cities which the princes of that house had adorned or strengthened. But in the history of their dynasty the name of the city chiefly stands out as the chosen place for the execution of princes whom it was convenient to put out of the way.

Here Crispus died at the bidding of Constantine, and Gallus at the bidding of Constantius. Under Theodoric, Pola doubtless shared that general prosperity of the Istrian land on which Cassiodorus grows eloquent when writing to its inhabitants. In the next generation Pola appears in somewhat of the same character which has come back to it in our own times; it was there that Belisarius gathered the Imperial fleet for his second and less prosperous expedition against the Gothic lords of Italy. But, after the break up of the Frankish Empire, the history of medieval Pola is but a history of decline. It was, in the geography of Dante, the furthest city of Italy; but, like most of the other cities of its own neighborhood, its day of greatness had passed away when Dante sang.

Tossed to and fro between the temporal and spiritual lords who claimed to be marquesses of Istria, torn by the dissensions of aristocratic and popular parties among its own citizens,

SEEING EUROPE WITH FAMOUS AUTHORS

Pola found rest, the rest of bondage, in submission to the dominion of Saint Mark in 1331.* Since then, till its new birth in our own times, Pola has been a failing city. Like the other Istrian and Dalmatian towns, modern revolutions have handed it over from Venice to Austria, from Austria to France, from France to Austria again. It is under its newest masters that Pola has at last begun to live a fresh life, and the haven whence Belisarius† sailed forth has again become a haven in more than name, the cradle of the rising navy of the united Austrian and Hungarian realm.

That haven is indeed a noble one. Few sights are more striking than to see the huge mass of the amphitheater at Pola seeming to rise at once out of the land-locked sea. As Pola is seen now, the amphitheater is the one monument of its older days, which strikes the eye in the general view, and which divides attention with signs that show how heartily the once forsaken city has entered on its new career. But in the old time Pola could show all the buildings which befitted its rank as a colony of Rome. The amphitheater, of course, stood without the walls; the city itself stood at the foot and on the slope of the hill which was crowned by the capitol of the colony, where the modern fortress rises above the Franciscan church. Parts of the Roman wall still stand; one of its gates is left; another has left a neighbor and a memory. . . .

---

*That is, of Venice.
†The famous general of the Emperor Justinian, reputed to have become blind and been neglected in his old age.

AUSTRIA'S ADRIATIC PORTS

Travelers are sometimes apt to complain, and that not wholly without reason, that all amphitheaters are very like one another. At Pola this remark is less true than elsewhere, as the amphitheater there has several marked peculiarities of its own. We do not pretend to expound all its details scientifically; but this we may say, that those who dispute—if the dispute still goes on—about various points as regards the Coliseum at Rome will do well to go and look for some further light in the amphitheater of Pola. The outer range, which is wonderfully perfect, while the inner arrangements are fearfully ruined, consists, on the side toward the town, of two rows of arches, with a third story with square-headed openings above them.

But the main peculiarity in the outside is to be found in four tower-like projections, not, as at Arles and Nîmes, signs of Saracenic occupation, but clearly parts of the original design. Many conjectures have been made about them; they look as if they were means of approach to the upper part of the building; but it is wisest not to be positive. But the main peculiarity of this amphitheater is that it lies on the slope of a hill, which thus supplied a natural basement for the seats on one side only. But this same position swallowed up the lower arcade on this side, and it hindered the usual works underneath the seats from being carried into this part of the building.

SPALATO*

BY EDWARD A. FREEMAN

The main object and center of all historical and architectural inquiries on the Dalmatian coast is, of course, the home of Diocletian, the still abiding palace of Spalato. From a local point of view, it is the spot which the greatest of the long line of renowned Illyrian Emperors chose as his resting-place from the toils of warfare and government, and where he reared the vastest and noblest dwelling that ever arose at the bidding of a single man. From an ecumenical point of view, Spalato is yet more. If it does not rank with Rome, Old and New, with Ravenna and with Trier, it is because it never was, like them, an actual seat of empire. But it not the less marks a stage, and one of the greatest stages, in the history of the Empire.

On his own Dalmatian soil, Docles of Salone, Diocletian of Rome, was the man who had won fame for his own land, and who, on the throne of the world, did not forget his provincial birthplace. In the sight of Rome and of the world Jovius Augustus was more than this. Alike in the history of politics and in the history of art, he has left his mark on all time that has come after him, and it is on his own Spalato that his mark has been most deeply stamped. The polity of Rome and the architecture of Rome alike received a new life at his hands. In each

*From "Sketches from the Subject and Neighbour Lands of Venice." Published by the Macmillan Co.

alike he cast away shams and pretenses, and made the true construction of the fabric stand out before men's eyes. Master of the Rome world, if not King, yet more than King, he let the true nature of his power be seen, and, first among the Cæsars, arrayed himself with the outward pomp of sovereignty.

In a smaller man we might have deemed the change a mark of weakness, a sign of childish delight in gewgaws, titles, and trappings. Such could hardly have been the motive in the man who, when he deemed that his work was done, could cast away both the form and the substance of power, and could so steadily withstand all temptations to take them up again. It was simply that the change was fully wrought; that the chief magistrate of the commonwealth had gradually changed into the sovereign of the Empire; that Imperator, Cæsar, and Augustus, once titles lowlier than that of King, had now become, as they have ever since remained, titles far loftier. The change was wrought, and all that Diocletian did was to announce the fact of the change to the world.

Nor did the organizing hand of Jovius confine its sphere to the polity of the Empire only. He built himself a house, and, above all builders, he might boast himself of the house that he had builded. Fast by his own birth-place—a meaner soul might have chosen some distant spot—Diocletian reared the palace which marks a still greater epoch in Roman art than his political changes mark in Roman polity. On the inmost shore of one of the lake-like inlets of the Hadriatic, an inlet guarded almost from sight by the great island of Bua at its mouth, lay his own Salona, now desolate, then one of the great cities of the Roman world. But it was not in the city, it was not close under its walls, that Diocletian fixt his home. An isthmus between the bay of Salona and the outer sea cuts off a peninsula, which again throws out two horns into the water to form the harbor which has for ages supplanted Salona.

There, not on any hill-top, but on a level spot by the coast, with the sea in front, with a background of more distant mountains, and with one peaked hill rising between the two seas like a watch-tower, did Diocletian build the house to which he withdrew when he deemed that his work of empire was over. And in building that house, he won for himself, or for the nameless genius whom he set at work, a place in the history of art worthy to rank alongside of Iktinos of Athens and Anthemios of Byzantium, of William of Durham and of Hugh of Lincoln.

And now the birthplace of Jovius is forsaken, but his house still abides, and abides in a shape marvelously little shorn of its ancient greatness. The name which it still bears comes straight from the name of the elder home of the Cæsars. The fates of the two spots have been in a strange way the converse of one another. By the banks of the Tiber the city of Romulus became the house of a single man; by the shores of the Hadriatic the house of a single man became a city. The Palatine hill became the Palatium of the Cæsars, and Palatium was the name which was borne by the house of

AUSTRIA'S ADRIATIC PORTS

Cæsar by the Dalmatian shore. The house became a city; but its name still clave to it, and the house of Jovius still, at least in the mouths of its own inhabitants, keeps its name in the slightly altered form of Spalato. . . .

We land with the moon lighting up the water, with the stars above us, the northern wain shining on the Hadriatic, as if, while Diocletian was seeking rest by Salona, the star of Constantine was rising over York and Trier. Dimly rising above us we see, disfigured indeed, but not destroyed, the pillared front of the palace, reminding us of the Tabularium of Rome's own capitol. We pass under gloomy arches, through dark passages and presently we find ourselves in the center of palace and city, between those two renowned rows of arches which mark the greatest of all epochs in the history of the building art. We think how the man who reorganized the Empire of Rome was also the man who first put harmony and consistency into the architecture of Rome. We think that, if it was in truth the crown of Diocletian which passed to every Cæsar from the first Constantius to the last Francis, it was no less in the pile which rose into being at his word that the germ was planted which grew into Pisa and Durham, into Westminster and Saint Ouen.

There is light enough to mark the columns put for the first time to their true Roman use, and to think how strange was the fate which called up on this spot the happy arrangement which had entered the brain of no earlier artist—the arrangement which, but a few years later, was to be applied to another use in the basilica of the Lateran and in Saint Paul Without the Walls. Yes, it is in the court of the persecutor, the man who boasted that he had wiped out the Christian superstition from the world, that we see the noblest forestalling of the long arcades of the Christian basilica.

It is with thoughts like these, thoughts pressing all the more upon us where every outline is clear and every detail is visible, that we tread for the first time the Court of Jovius—the columns with their arches on either side of us, the vast bell-tower rising to the sky, as if to mock the art of those whose mightiest works might still seem only to grovel upon earth. Nowhere within the compass of the Roman world do we find ourselves more distinctly in the presence of one of the great minds of the world's history; we see that, alike in politics and in art, Diocletian breathed a living soul into a lifeless body. In the bitter irony of the triumphant faith, his mausoleum has become a church, his temple has become a baptistery, the great bell-tower rises proudly over his own work; his immediate dwelling-place is broken down and crowded with paltry houses; but the sea-front and the Golden Gate are still there amid all disfigurements, and the great peristyle stands almost unhurt, to remind us of the greatest advance that a single mind ever made in the progress of the building art.

At the present time the city into which the house of Diocletian has grown is the largest and most growing town of the Dalmatian coast. It has had to yield both spiritual and temporal

AUSTRIA'S ADRIATIC PORTS

precedence to Zara, but, both in actual population and all that forms the life of a city, Spalato greatly surpasses Zara and all its other neighbors. The youngest Dalmatian towns, which could boast neither of any mythical origin nor of any Imperial foundation, the city which, as it were, became a city by mere chance, has outstript the colonies of Epidauros, of Corinth, and of Rome.

The palace of Diocletian had but one occupant; after the founder no Emperor had dwelled in it, unless we hold that this was the villa near Salona where the deposed Emperor Nepos was slain, during the patriciate of Odoacer. The forsaken palace seems, while still almost new, to have become a cloth factory, where women worked, and which therefore appears in the "Notitia" as a Gynæcium. But when Salona was overthrown, the palace stood ready to afford shelter to those who were driven from their homes. The palace, in the widest sense of the word—for of course its vast circuit took in quarters for soldiers and officials of various kinds, as well as the rooms actually occupied by the Emperor—stood ready to become a city.

It was a chester ready made, with its four streets, its four gates, all but that toward the sea flanked with octagonal towers, and with four greater square towers at the corners. To this day the circuit of the walls is nearly perfect; and the space contained within them must be as large as that contained within some of the oldest chesters in our own island. The walls, the towers, the gates, are those of a city rather than of a

23

house. Two of the gates, tho their towers are gone, are nearly perfect; the "porta aurea," with its graceful ornaments; the "porta ferrea" in its stern plainness, strangely crowned with its small campanile of later days perched on its top. Within the walls, besides the splendid buildings which still remain, besides the broken-down walls and chambers which formed the immediate dwelling-place of the founder, the main streets were lined with massive arcades, large parts of which still remain.

Diocletian, in short, in building a house, had built a city. In the days of Constantine Porphyrogenitus it was a "Κάστρον"—Greek and English had by his day alike borrowed the Latin name; but it was a "Κάστρον" which Diocletian had built as his own house, and within which was his hall and palace. In his day the city bore the name of Aspalathon, which he explains to mean "little palace." When the palace had thus become a common habitation of men, it is not wonderful that all the more private buildings whose use had passed away were broken down, disfigured, and put to mean uses.

The work of building over the site must have gone on from that day to this. The view in Wheeler shows several parts of the enclosure occupied by ruins which are now covered with houses. The real wonder is that so much has been spared and has survived to our own days. And we are rather surprised to find Constantine saying that in his time the greater part had been destroyed. For the parts which must always have been the stateliest remain still.

AUSTRIA'S ADRIATIC PORTS

The great open court, the peristyle, with its arcades, have become the public plaza of the town; the mausoleum on one side of it and the temple on the other were preserved and put to Christian uses.

We say the mausoleum, for we fully accept the suggestion made by Professor Glavinich, the curator of the museum of Spalato, that the present duomo, traditionally called the Temple of Jupiter, was not a temple, but a mausoleum. These must have been the great public buildings of the palace, and, with the addition of the bell-tower, they remain the chief public buildings of the modern city. But, tho the ancient square of the palace remains wonderfully perfect, the modern city, with its Venetian defenses, its Venetian and later buildings, has spread itself far beyond the walls of Diocletian. But those walls have made the history of Spalato, and it is the great buildings which stand within them that give Spalato its special place in the history of architecture.

RAGUSA*

BY HARRY DE WINDT

Viewed from the sea, and at first sight, the place somewhat resembles Monte Carlo with its white villas, palms, and background of rugged, gray hills. But this is the modern portion of the town, outside the fortifications,

*From "Through Savage Europe." Published by J. B. Lippincott Co.

erected many centuries ago. Within them lies the real Ragusa—a wonderful old city which teems with interest, for its time-worn buildings and picturesque streets recall, at every turn, the faded glories of this "South Slavonic Athens." A bridge across the moat which protects the old city is the link between the present and past. In new Ragusa you may sit on the crowded esplanade of a fashionable watering place; but pass through a frowning archway into the old town, and, save in the main street, which has modern shops and other up-to-date surroundings, you might be living in the dark ages. For as far back as in the ninth century Ragusa was the capital of Dalmatia and an independent republic, and since that period her literary and commercial triumphs, and the tragedies she has survived in the shape of sieges, earthquakes, and pestilence, render the records of this little-known state almost as engrossing as those of ancient Rome.

Until I came here I had pictured a squalid Eastern place, devoid of ancient or modern interest; most of my fellow-countrymen probably do likewise, nothwithstanding the fact that when London was a small and obscure town Ragusa was already an important center of commerce and civilization. The republic was always a peaceful one, and its people excelled in trade and the fine arts. Thus, as early as the fourteenth century the Ragusan fleet was the envy of the world; its vessels were then known as Argusas to British mariners, and the English word "Argosy" is probably derived from the name.

AUSTRIA'S ADRIATIC PORTS

These tiny ships went far afield—to the Levant and Northern Europe, and even to the Indies—a voyage frought, in those days, with much peril. At this epoch Ragusa had achieved a mercantile prosperity unequalled throughout Europe, but in later years the greater part of the fleet joined and perished with the Spanish Armada.

And this catastrophe was the precursor of a series of national disasters. In 1667 the city was laid waste by an earthquake which killed over twenty thousand people, and this was followed by a terrible visitation of the plague, which further decimated the population. Ragusa, however, was never a large city, and even at its zenith, in the sixteenth century, it numbered under forty thousand souls, and now contains only about a third of that number.

In 1814 the Vienna Congress finally deprived the republic of its independence, and it became (with Dalmatia) an Austrian possession. Trade has not increased here of recent years, as in Herzegovina and Bosnia. The harbor, at one time one of the most important ports in Europe, is too small and shallow for modern shipping, and the oil industry, once the backbone of the place, has sadly dwindled of late years.

Ragusa itself now having no harbor worthy of the name, the traveler by sea must land at Gravosa about a mile north of the old city. Gravosa is merely a suburb of warehouses, shipping, and sailor-men, as unattractive as the London Docks, and the Hotel Petko swarmed with mosquitoes and an animal which seems to thrive and flourish throughout the Balkan States—the rat.

The old Custom House is perhaps the most beautiful building in Ragusa, and is one of the few which survived the terrible earthquake of 1667. The structure bears the letters "I. H. S." over the principal entrance in commemoration of this fact. Its courtyard is a dream of beauty, and the stone galleries around it are surrounded with inscriptions of great age.

Ragusa is a Slav town, but altho the name of streets appear in Slavonic characters, Italian is also spoken on every side and the "Stradone," with its arcades and narrow precipitous alleys at right angles, is not unlike a street in Naples. The houses are built in small blocks, as a protection against earthquakes—the terror of every Ragusan (only mention the word and he will cross himself)—and here on a fine Sunday morning you may see Dalmatians, Albanians, and Herzegovinians in their gaudiest finery, while here and there a wild-eyed Montenegrin, armed to the teeth, surveys the gay scene with a scowl, of shyness rather than ill-humor.

Outside the café, on the Square (where flocks of pigeons whirl around as at St. Mark's in Venice), every little table is occupied; but here the women are gowned in the latest Vienna fashions, and Austrian uniforms predominate. And the sun shines as warmly as in June (on this 25th day of March), and the cathedral bells chime a merry accompaniment to a military band; a sky of the brightest blue gladdens the eye, fragrant flowers the senses, and the traveler sips his bock or mazagran, and thanks his stars he is not spending the winter in cold, foggy England. Refreshments are served by a white-aproned garçon, and street boys are selling the "Daily Mail" and "Gil Blas," just as they are on the far-away boulevards of Paris.

CATTARO*

BY EDWARD A. FREEMAN

The end of a purely Dalmatian pilgrimage will be Cattaro. He who goes further along the coast will pass into lands that have a history, past and present, which is wholly distinct from that of the coast which he has hitherto traced from Zara—we might say from Capo d'Istria—onward. We have not reached the end of the old Venetian dominion—for that we must carry our voyage to Crete and Cyprus. But we have reached the end of the nearly continuous Venetian dominion—the end of the coast which, save at two small points, was either Venetian or Regusan—the end of that territory of the two maritime commonwealths which they kept down to their fall in modern times, and in which they have been succeeded by the modern Dalmatian kingdom. . . .

The city stands at the end of an inlet of the sea fifteen or twenty miles long, and it has mountains around it so high that it is only in fair summer weather that the sun can be

*From "Sketches from the Subject and Neighbour Lands of Venice." Published by the Macmillan Co.

seen; in winter Cattaro never enjoys his presence. There certainly is no place where it is harder to believe that the smooth waters of the narrow, lake-like inlet, with mountains on each side which it seems as if one could put out one's hand and touch, are really part of the same sea which dashes against the rocks of Ragusa. They end in a meadow-like coast ch makes one think of Bourget or Trasienus rather than of Hadria. The Dalmatian voyage is well ended by the sail along the Bocche, the loveliest piece of inland sea which can be conceived, and whose shores are as rich in curious bits of political history as they are in scenes of surpassing natural beauty.

The general history of the district consists in the usual tossing to and fro between the various powers which have at different times been strong in the neighborhood. Cattaro was in the reign of Basil the Macedonian besieged and taken by Saracens, who presently went on unsuccessfully to besiege Ragusa. And, as under Byzantine rule it was taken by Saracens, so under Venetian rule it was more than once besieged by Turks. In the intermediate stages we get the usual alternations of independence and of subjection to all the neighboring powers in turn, till in 1419 Cattaro finally became Venetian. At the fall of the republic it became part of the Austrian share of the spoil. When the spoilers quarreled, it fell to France. When England, Russia, and Montenegro were allies, the city joined the land of which it naturally forms the head, and Cattaro became the Montenegrin haven and capital. When

AUSTRIA'S ADRIATIC PORTS

France was no longer dangerous, and the powers of Europe came together to parcel out other men's goods, Austria calmly asked for Cattaro back again, and easily got it.

In the city of Cattaro the Orthodox Church is still in a minority, but it is a minority not far short of a majority. Outside its walls, the Orthodox outnumber the Catholics. In short, when we reach Cattaro, we have very little temptation to fancy ourselves in Italy or in any part of Western Christendom. We not only know, but feel, that we are on the Byzantine side of the Hadriatic; that we have, in fact, made our way into Eastern Europe.

And East and West, Slav and Italian, New Rome and Old, might well struggle for the possession of the land and of the water through which we pass from Ragusa to our final goal at Cattaro. The strait leads us into a gulf; another narrow strait leads us into an inner gulf; and on an inlet again branching out of that inner gulf lies the furthest of Dalmatian cities. The lower city, Cattaro itself, seems to lie so quietly, so peacefully, as if in a world of its own from which nothing beyond the shores of its own Bocche could enter, that we are tempted to forget, not only that the spot has been the scene of so many revolutions through so many ages, but that it is even now a border city, a city on the marchland of contending powers, creeds, and races. . . .

The city of Cattaro itself is small, standing on a narrow ledge between the gulf and the base of the mountain. It carries the features of the Dalmatian cities to what any one who has not seen Traü will call their extreme point. But, tho the streets of Cattaro are narrow, yet they are civilized and airy-looking compared with those of Traü, and the little paved squares, as so often along this coast, suggest the memory of the ruling city.

The memory of Venice is again called up by the graceful little scraps of its characteristic architecture which catch the eye ever and anon among the houses of Cattaro. The landing-place, the marina, the space between the coast and the Venetian wall, where we pass for the last time under the winged lion over the gate, has put on the air of a boulevard. But the forms and costume of Bocchesi and Montenegrins, the men of the gulf, with their arms in their girdles, no less than the men of the black mountain, banish all thought that we are anywhere but where we really are, at one of the border points of Christian and civilized Europe. If in the sons of the mountains we see the men who have in all ages held out against the invading Turk, we see in their brethren of the coast the men who, but a few years back, brought Imperial, Royal, and Apostolic Majesty to its knees. . . .

At Cattaro the Orthodox Church is on its own ground, standing side by side on equal terms with its Latin rival, pointing to lands where the Filioque* is unknown and where the Bishop of the Old Rome has even been deemed an intruder. The building itself is a small Byzantine church, less Byzantine in fact in its

---

*That is, lands where the Greek Church prevails.

AUSTRIA'S ADRIATIC PORTS

outline than the small churches of the Byzantine type at Zara, Spalato, and Traü. The single dome rises, not from the intersection of a Greek cross, but from the middle of a single body, and, resting as it does on pointed arches, it suggests the thought of Périgueux and Angoulême. But this arrangement, which is shared by a neighboring Latin church, is well known throughout the East.

The Latin duomo, which has been minutely described by Mr. Neale,* is of quite another type, and is by no means Dalmatian in its general look. A modern west front with two western towers does not go for much; but it reminds us that a design of the same kind was begun at Traü in better times. The inside is quite unlike anything of later Italian work.

The traveler whose objects are of a more general kind turns away from this border church of Christendom as the last stage of a pilgrimage unsurpassed either for natural beauty or for historic interest. And, as he looks up at the mountain which rises almost close above the east end of the duomo of Cattaro, and thinks of the land† and the men to which the path over that mountain leads, he feels that, on this frontier at least, the spirit still lives which led English warriors to the side of Manuel Komnênos, and which steeled the heart of the last Constantine to die in the breach for the Roman name and the faith of Christendom.

*John Mason Neale, author of "An Introduction to the History of the Holy Eastern Church."

†Montenegro.

VIII

OTHER AUSTRIAN SCENES

CRACOW*

BY MÉNIE MURIEL DOWIE

Cracow, old, tired and dispirited, speaks and thinks only of the ruinous past. When you drive into Cracow from the station for the first time, you are breathless, smiling, and tearful all at once; in the great Ring-platz—a mass of old buildings—Cracow seems to hold out her arms to you—those long sides that open from the corner where the cab drives in. You do not have time to notice separately the row of small trees down on one side, beneath which bright-colored women-figures control their weekly market; you do not notice the sort of courthouse in the middle with its red roof, cream-colored galleries and shops beneath; you do not notice the great tall church at one side of brick and stone most perfectly time-reconciled, or the houses, or the crazed paving, or the innocent little groups of cabs—you only see Cracow holding out her arms to you, and you may lean down your head and weep from pure instinctive sympathy.

*From "A Girl in the Karpathians." After publishing this book, Miss Dowie became the wife of Henry Norman, the author and traveler.

SEEING EUROPE WITH FAMOUS AUTHORS

Suddenly a choir of trumpets breaks out into a chorale from the big church tower; the melancholy of it I shall never forget—the very melody seemed so old and tired, so worn and sweet and patient, like Cracow. Those trumpet notes have mourned in that tower for hundreds of years. It is the Hymn of Timeless Sorrow that they play, and the key to which they are attuned in Cracow's long despair. Hush! That is her voice, the old town's voice, high and sad—she is speaking to you.

Dear Cracow! Never again it seems to me, shall I come so near to the deathless hidden sentiment of Poland as in those first moments. It would be no use to tell her to take heart, that there may be brighter days coming, and so forth. Lemberg may feel so, Lemberg that has the feelings of any other big new town, the strength and the determination; but Cracow's day was in the long ago, as a gay capital, a brilliant university town full of princes, of daring, of culture, of wit. She has outlived her day, and can only mourn over what has been and the times that she has seen; she may be always proud of her character, of the brave blood that has made scarlet her streets, but she can never be happy remodeled as an Austrian garrison town, and in the new Poland—the Poland whose foundation stones are laid in the hearts of her people, and that may yet be built some day—in that new Poland there will be no place for aristocratic, high-bred Cracow.

During my stay in the beautiful butter-colored palace that is now a hotel, I went round the museums, galleries, and universities, most if not all of which are free to the public. It would be unfair to give the idea that Cracow has completely fallen to decay. This is not the case. Austria has erected some very handsome buildings; and a town with such fine pictures, good museums, and two universities, can not be complained of as moribund. At the same time, I can only record faithfully my impression, and that was that everything new, everything modern, was hopelessly out of tone in Cracow; progress, which, tho desirable, may be a vulgar thing, would not suit her, and does not seem at home in her streets.

About the Florian's Thor, with its round towers of old, sorrel-colored brick, and the Czartoryski Museum, there is nothing to say that the guide-book would not say better. In the museum, a tattered Polish flag of red silk, with the white eagle, a cheerful bird with curled tail, opened mouth, chirping defiantly to the left, imprest me, and a portrait of Szopen (Chopin) in fine profile when laid out dead. For amusement, there was a Paul Potter bull beside a Paul Potter willow, delightfully unconscious of a coming Paul Potter thunderstorm, and a miniature of Shakespeare which did not resemble any of the portraits of him that I am familiar with. Any amount of Turkish trappings and reminiscences of Potocki and Kosciuszko, of course. As I had no guide-book, I am quite prepared to learn that I overlooked the most important relics.

In the cathedral, away up on the hill of Wawel, above the river Vistula (Wisla) I prowled about among the crypts with a curious specimen

OTHER AUSTRIAN SCENES

of beadledom who ran off long unintelligible histories in atrocious Viennese patois about every solemn tomb by which we stood. So far as I was concerned it might just as well have been the functionary who herds small droves of visitors in Westminster Abbey. I never listen to these people, because (1) I do not care to be informed; and (2) since I should never remember what they said, it is useless my even letting it in at one ear. The kindly, cobwebby old person who piloted me among those wonderful kings' graves in Cracow was personally not uninteresting, indeed a fine study, and his rigmaroles brought up infallibly upon three words which I could not fail to notice: these were "silberner Sarg vergoldet" (silver coffin, gilded). It had an odd fascination for me this phrase, as I stood always waiting for it; why, I wondered, should anybody want to gild a good solid silver coffin?

At the time of my first visit, the excavation necessary to form the crypt for the resting-place of Mickiewicz* was in progress, and I went in among the limey, dusty workmen, with their tallow candles, and looked round. In return for my gulden, the beadle gave me a few immortelles from Sobieski's tomb, and some laurel leaves from Kosciuszko's; and remembering friends at home of refinedly ghoulish tastes, I determined to preserve those poor moldering fragments for them.

Most of my days and evenings I spent wandering by the Vistula and in and out of the

*One of Poland's greatest poets.

hundred churches. My plan was to sight a spire, and then walk to the root of it, so to speak. In this manner I saw the town very well. The houses were of brick and plaster, the rich carmine-red brick that has made Cracow so beautiful. On each was a beautiful façade, and pediments in renaissance, bas-relief work of cupids, and classic figures with ribands and roses tying among them, seeming to speak, somehow, of the dead princes and the mighty aristocracy which had cost Cracow so dear.

In the Jews' quarter that loud lifelong market of theirs was going forward, which required seemingly only some small basinfuls of sour Gurken and a few spoonfuls of beans of its stock-in-trade. Mingling among the Jews were the peasants, of course; the men in tightly fitting trousers of white blanket cloth, rich embroidered on the upper part and down the seams in blue and red; the women wearing pink printed muslin skirts, often with a pale blue muslin apron and a lemon-colored fine wool cloth, spotted in pink, upon the head. They manifested a great appreciation of color, but none of form, and after the free dress of the Hucal women, these people, mummied in their red tartan shawls—all hybrid Stewarts, they seemed to me—were merely bright bundles in the sunshine.

In the shops in Cracow, French was nearly always the language of attack, and a good deal was spoken in the hotel. I had occasion to buy a great many things, but, according to my custom, not a photograph was among them; therefore, when I go back, I shall receive per-

OTHER AUSTRIAN SCENES

fectly new and fresh impressions of the place, and can cherish no vague memories, encouraged by an album at home, in which the nameless cathedrals of many countries confuse themselves, and only the Coliseum at Rome stands forth, not to be contradicted or misnamed.

But it became necessary to put a period to my wandering, unless I wished to find myself stranded in Vienna with "neither cross nor pile." The references to money-matters have been designedly slight throughout these pages. It is not my habit to keep accounts. I have never found that you get any money back by knowing just how you have spent it, and a conscience-pricking record of expenses is very ungrateful reading. So, when a certain beautiful evening came, I felt that I had to look upon it as my last. Being too early for the train, I bid the man drive about in the early summer dark for three-quarters of an hour.

To such as do not care for precise information and statistics in foreign places, but appreciate rather atmosphere and impression, I can recommend this course. In and out among the pretty garden woods, outside the town, we drove. Buildings loomed majestically out of the night; sometimes it was the tower of an unknown church, sometimes it was the house of some forgotten family that sprang suggestively to the eye, and I was grateful that I was left to suppose the indefinite type of Austrian bureau, which occupied, in all probability, the first floor. Then we came to the river, and later, Wawel stood massed out black upon the blue, the glorious gravestone of a fallen Power.

All the stars were shining, and little red-yellow lights in the castle windows were not much bigger. Above the whisper of the willows on its bank came the deep, quiet murmur of the Vistula, and every now and then, over the several towers of the solemn old palaces and the spires of the church where Poland has laid her kings, and so recently the king of the poets, the stars were dropping from their places, like sudden spiders, letting themselves down into the vast by faint yellow threads that showed a moment after the star itself was gone.

Later, as I looked from the open gallery of the train that was taking me away, I could not help thinking that, just a hundred years ago, Wawel's star was shining with a light bright enough for all Europe to see; but even as the stars fell that night and left their places empty, so Wawel's star has fallen and Poland's star has fallen too.

ON THE ROAD TO PRAGUE*

BY BAYARD TAYLOR

I was pleasantly disappointed on entering Bohemia. Instead of a dull, uninteresting country, as I expected, it is a land full of the most lovely scenery. There is everything which can gratify the eye—high blue mountains, valleys of the sweetest pastoral look and romantic old ruins. The very name of Bohemia is as-

*From "Views Afoot." Published by G. P. Putnam's Sons.

sociated with wild and wonderful legends of the rude barbaric ages. Even the chivalric tales of the feudal times of Germany grow tame beside these earlier and darker histories. The fallen fortresses of the Rhine or the robber-castles of the Odenwald had not for me so exciting an interest as the shapeless ruins cumbering these lonely mountains. The civilized Saxon race was left behind; I saw around me the features and heard the language of one of those rude Slavonic tribes whose original home was on the vast steppes of Central Asia.

I have rarely enjoyed traveling more than our first two days' journey toward Prague. The range of the Erzgebirge ran along on our right; the snow still lay in patches upon it, but the valleys between, with their little clusters of white cottages, were green and beautiful. About six miles before reaching Teplitz we passed Kulm, the great battlefield which in a measure decided the fate of Napoleon. He sent Vandamme with forty thousand men to attack the allies before they could unite their forces, and thus effect their complete destruction. Only the almost despairing bravery of the Russian guards under Ostermann, who held him in check till the allied troops united, prevented Napoleon's design. At the junction of the roads, where the fighting was hottest, the Austrians have erected a monument to one of their generals. Not far from it is that of Prussia, simple and tasteful. A woody hill near, with the little village of Kulm at its foot, was the station occupied by Vandamme at the commencement of the battle. There is now a beautiful chapel on its summit which can be seen far and wide. A little distance farther the Czar of Russia has erected a third monument, to the memory of the Russians who fell. Four lions rest on the base of the pedestal, and on the top of the shaft, forty-five feet high, Victory is represented as engraving the date, "Aug. 30, 1813," on a shield. The dark pine-covered mountains on the right overlook the whole field and the valley of Torlitz; Napoleon rode along their crests several days after the battle to witness the scene of his defeat.

Teplitz lies in a lovely valley, several miles wide, bounded by the Bohemian mountains on one side and the Erzgebirge on the other. One straggling peak near is crowned with a picturesque ruin, at whose foot the spacious bath-buildings lie half hidden in foliage. As we went down the principal street I noticed nearly every house was a hotel; we learned afterward that in summer the usual average of visitors is five thousand.* The waters resemble those of the celebrated Carlsbad; they are warm and practically efficacious in rheumatism and diseases of like character. After leaving Teplitz the road turned to the east, toward a lofty mountain which we had seen the morning before. The peasants, as they passed by, saluted us with "Christ greet you!"

We stopt for the night at the foot of the peak called the Milleschauer, and must have ascended nearly two thousand feet, for we had a wide view the next morning, altho the mists

*The population now (1914) is 24,000.

OTHER AUSTRIAN SCENES

and clouds hid the half of it. The weather being so unfavorable, we concluded not to ascend, and descended through green fields and orchards snowy with blossoms to Lobositz, on the Elbe. Here we reached the plains again, where everything wore the luxuriance of summer; it was a pleasant change from the dark and rough scenery we left.

The road passed through Theresienstadt, the fortress of Northern Bohemia. The little city is surrounded by a double wall and moat which can be filled with water, rendering it almost impossible to be taken. In the morning we were ferried over the Moldau, and after journeying nearly all day across barren, elevated plains saw, late in the afternoon, the sixty-seven spires of Prague below.

I feel out of the world in this strange, fantastic, yet beautiful, old city. We have been rambling all morning through its winding streets, stopping sometimes at a church to see the dusty tombs and shrines or to hear the fine music which accompanies the morning mass. I have seen no city yet that so forcibly reminds one of the past and makes him forget everything but the associates connected with the scenes around him. The language adds to the illusion. Three-fourths of the people in the streets speak Bohemian and many of the signs are written in the same tongue.

The palace of the Bohemian kings still looks down on the city from the western heights, and their tombs stand in the cathedral of St. John. When one has climbed up the stone steps leading to the fortress, there is a glorious prospect before him. Prague with its spires and towers lies in the valleys below, through which curves the Moldau with its green islands, disappearing among the hills which enclose the city on every side. The fantastic Byzantine architecture of many of the churches and towers gives the city a peculiar Oriental appearance; it seems to have been transported from the hills of Syria. . . .

Having found out first a few of the locations, we haunted our way with difficulty through its labyrinths, seeking out every place of note or interest. Reaching the bridge at last, we concluded to cross over and ascend to the Hradschin, the palace of the Bohemian kings. The bridge was commenced in 1357, and was one hundred and fifty years in building. That was the way the old Germans did their work, and they made a structure which will last a thousand years longer. Every pier is surmounted with groups of saints and martyrs, all so worn and timebeaten that there is little left of their beauty, if they ever had any. The most important of them—at least to Bohemians—is that of St. John Nepomuk, now considered as the patron-saint of the land. He was a priest many centuries ago [1340–1393] whom one of the kings threw from the bridge into the Moldau because he refused to reveal to him what the queen confest. The legend says the body swam for some time on the river with five stars around its head.

Ascending the broad flight of steps to the Hradschin, I paused a moment to look at the scene below. A slight blue haze hung over the

OTHER AUSTRIAN SCENES

clustering towers, and the city looked dim through it, like a city seen in a dream. It was well that it should so appear, for not less dim and misty are the memories that haunt its walls. There was no need of a magician's wand to bid that light cloud shadow forth the forms of other times. They came uncalled for even by Fancy. Far, far back in the past I saw the warrior-princess who founded the kingly city—the renowned Libussa, whose prowess and talent inspired the women of Bohemia to rise at her death and storm the land that their sex might rule where it obeyed before. On the mountain opposite once stood the palace of the bloody Wlaska, who reigned with her Amazon band for seven years over half Bohemia. Those streets below had echoed with the fiery words of Huss, and the castle of his follower— the blind Ziska, who met and defeated the armies of the German Empire—molders on the mountains above. Many a year of war and tempest has passed over the scene. The hills around have borne the armies of Wallenstein and Frederick the Great; the war-cry of Bavaria, Sweden and Poland has echoed in the valley, and the red glare of the midnight cannon or the flames of burning palaces have often gleamed along the "blood-dyed waters" of the Moldau. . . .

On the way down again we stept into the St. Nicholas Church, which was built by the Jesuits. The interior has a rich effect, being all of brown and gold. The massive pillars are made to resemble reddish-brown marble, with gilded capitals, and the statues at the base are profusely ornamented in the same style. The music chained me there a long time. There was a grand organ, assisted by a full orchestra and large choir of singers. It was placed above, and at every sound of the priest's bell the flourish of trumpets and deep roll of the drums filled the dome with a burst of quivering sound, while the giant pipes of the organ breathed out their full harmony and the very air shook under the peal. It was like a triumphal strain. The soul became filled with thoughts of power and glory; every sense was changed into one dim, indistinct emotion of rapture which held the spirit as if spellbound.

Not far from this place is the palace of Wallenstein, in the same condition as when he inhabited it. It is a plain, large building having beautiful gardens attached to it, which are open to the public. We went through the courtyard, threaded a passage with a roof of rough stalactitic rock and entered the garden, where a revolving fountain was casting up its glittering arches.

THE CAVE OF ADELSBERG*

BY GEORGE STILLMAN HILLARD

The night had been passed at Adelsberg, and the morning had been agreeably occupied in exploring the wonders of its celebrated cavern. The entrance is through an opening in the side of a hill. In a few moments, after walking

*From "Six Months in Italy." Published by Houghton, Mifflin Co.

OTHER AUSTRIAN SCENES

down a gentle descent, a sound of flowing water is heard, and the light of the torches borne by the guides gleams faintly upon a river which runs through these sunless chasms, and revisits the glimpses of day at Planina, some ten miles distant.

The visitor now finds himself in a vast hall, walled and roofed by impenetrable darkness. of the stream, which is crossed by a wooden bridge; and the ascent on the other side is made by a similar flight of steps. The bridge and steps are marked by a double row of lights, which present a most striking appearance as their tremulous luster struggles through the night that broods over them. Such a scene recalls Milton's sublime pictures of Pandemonium, and shows directly to the eye what effects a great imaginative painter may produce with no other colors than light and darkness. Here are the "stately height," the "ample spaces," the "arched roof," the rows of "starry lamps and blazing cressets" of Satan's hall of council; and by the excited fancy the dim distance is easily peopled with gigantic forms and filled with the "rushing of congregated wings."

After this, one is led through a variety of chambers, differing in size and form, but essentially similar in character, and the attention is invited to the innumerable multitude of striking and fantastic objects which have been formed in the lapse of ages, by the mere dropping of water. Pendants hang from the roof, stalagmites grow from the floor like petrified stumps, and pillars and buttresses are disposed as oddly as in the architecture of a dream. Here, we are told to admire a bell, and there, a throne; here, a pulpit, and there, a butcher's shop; here, "the two hearts," and there, a fountain frozen into alabaster; and in every case we assent to the resemblance in the unquestioning mood of Polonius. One of the chambers, or halls, is used every year as a ball-room, for which purpose it has every requisite except an elastic floor, even to a natural dais for the orchestra.

Here, with the sort of pride with which a book collector shows a Mazarin Bible or a folio Shakespeare, the guides point out a beautiful piece of limestone which hangs from the roof in folds as delicate as a Cashmere shawl, to which the resemblance is made more exact by a well-defined border of deeper color than the web. Through this translucent curtain the light shines as through a picture in porcelain, and one must be very unimpressible not to bestow the tribute of admiration which is claimed. These are the trivial details which may be remembered and described, but the general effect produced by the darkness, the silence, the vast spaces, the innumerable forms, the vaulted roofs, the pillars and galleries melting away in the gloom like the long-drawn aisles of a cathedral, may be recalled but not communicated.

To see all these marvels requires much time, and I remained under ground long enough to have a new sense of the blessing of light. The first glimpse of returning day seen through the distant entrance brought with it an exhilarating sense of release, and the blue sky and cheerful sunshine were welcomed like the faces of long absent friends.

OTHER AUSTRIAN SCENES

A cave like that of Adelsberg—for all limestone caves are, doubtless, essentially similar in character—ought by all means to be seen if it comes in one's way, because it leaves impressions upon the mind unlike those derived from any other object. Nature stamps upon most of her operations a certain character of gravity and majesty. Order and symmetry attend upon her steps, and unity in variety is the law by which her movements are guided. But, beneath the surface of the earth, she seems a frolicsome child, or a sportive undine, who wreaths the unmanageable stone into weird and quaint forms, seemingly from no other motive than pure delight in the exercise of overflowing power. Everything is playful, airy, and fantastic; there is no spirit of soberness; no reference to any ulterior end; nothing from which food, fuel, or raiment can be extracted. These chasms have been scooped out, and these pillars have been reared, in the spirit in which the bird sings, or the kitten plays with the falling leaves. From such scenes we may safely infer that the plan of the Creator comprehends something more than material utility, that beauty is its own vindicator and interpreter, that sawmills were not the ultimate cause of mountain streams, nor wine-bottles of cork-trees.

THE MONASTERY OF MÖLK*

BY THOMAS FROGNALL DIBDIN

We had determined upon dining at Mölk the next day. The early morning was somewhat inauspicious; but as the day advanced, it grew bright and cheerful. Some delightful glimpses of the Danube, to the left, from the more elevated parts of the road, accompanied us the whole way, till we caught the first view, beneath a bright blue sky, of the towering church and Monastery of Mölk.

Conceive what you please, and yet you shall not conceive the situation of this monastery. Less elevated above the road than Chremsminster, but of a more commanding style of architecture, and of considerably greater extent, it strikes you—as the Danube winds round and washes its rocky base—as one of the noblest edifices in the world. The wooded heights of the opposite side of the Danube crown the view of this magnificent edifice, in a manner hardly to be surpassed. There is also a beautiful play of architectural lines and ornament in the front of the building, indicative of a pure Italian taste, and giving to the edifice, if not the air of towering grandeur, at least of dignified splendor. . . .

As usual, I ordered a late dinner, intending to pay my respects to the Principal, and obtain permission to inspect the library. My late monastic visits had inspired me with confidence; and I marched up the steep sides of the hill, upon which the monastery is built, quite assured of the suc-

*From "A Bibliographical, Antiquarian and Picturesque Tour," published in 1821.

OTHER AUSTRIAN SCENES

cess of the visit I was about to pay. You must now accompany the bibliographer to the monastery. In five minutes from entering the outer gate of the first quadrangle—looking toward Vienna, and which is the more ancient part of the building—I was in conversation with the Vice-Principal and Librarian, each of us speaking Latin. I delivered the letter which I had received at Salzburg, and proceeded to the library.

The view from this library is really enchanting, and put everything seen from a similar situation at Landshut and almost even at Chremsminster, out of my recollection. You look down upon the Danube, catching a fine sweep of the river, as it widens in its course toward Vienna. A man might sit, read, and gaze—in such a situation—till he fancied he had scarcely one earthly want! I now descended a small staircase, which brought me directly into the large library—forming the right wing of the building, looking up the Danube toward Lintz. I had scarcely uttered three notes of admiration, when the Abbé Strattman entered; and to my surprise and satisfaction, addrest me by name. We immediately commenced an ardent unintermitting conversation in the French language, which the Abbé speaks fluently and correctly.

I now took a leisurely survey of the library; which is, beyond all doubt, the finest room of its kind which I have seen upon the Continent—not for its size, but for its style of architecture, and the materials of which it is composed. I was told that it was "the Imperial Library in miniature," —but with this difference, let me here add, in favor of Mölk—that it looks over a magnificently-wooded country, with the Danube rolling its rapid course at its base. The wainscot and shelves are walnut tree, of different shades, inlaid, or dovetailed, surmounted by gilt ornaments. The pilasters have Corinthian capitals of gilt; and the bolder or projecting parts of a gallery, which surrounds the room, are covered with the same metal. Everything is in harmony. This library may be about a hundred feet in length, by forty in width. It is sufficiently well furnished with books, of the ordinary useful class, and was once, I suspect, much richer in the bibliographical lore of the fifteenth century.

On reaching the last descending step, just before entering the church, the Vice-Principal bade me look upward and view the corkscrew staircase. I did so; and to view and admire was one and the same operation of the mind. It was the most perfect and extraordinary thing of the kind which I had ever seen—the consummation, as I was told, of that particular species of art. The church is the very perfection of ecclesiastical Roman architecture; that of Chremsminster, altho fine, being much inferior to it in loftiness and richness of decoration. The windows are fixt so as to throw their concentrated light beneath a dome, of no ordinary height, and of no ordinary elegance of decoration; but this dome is suffering from damp, and the paintings upon the ceiling will, unless repaired, be effaced in the course of a few years.

The church is in the shape of a cross; and at the end of each of the transepts, is a rich altar, with statuary, in the style of art usual about a century ago. The pews—made of dark mahogany or walnut tree, much after the English fashion, but lower and more tasteful—are placed on each side of the nave, or entering; with ample space between them. They are exclusively appropriated to the tenants of the monastery. At the end of the nave, you look to the left, opposite—and observe, placed in a recess—a pulpit, which, from top to bottom, is completely covered with gold. And yet, there is nothing gaudy or tasteless, or glaringly obtrusive, in this extraordinary clerical rostrum. The whole is in the most perfect taste; and perhaps more judgment was required to manage such an ornament, or appendage—consistently with the splendid style of decoration exacted by the founder, for it was expressly the Prelate Dietmayr's wish that it should be so adorned,—than may on first consideration be supposed. In fact, the whole church is in a blaze of gold; and I was told that the gilding alone cost upward of ninety thousand florins. Upon the whole, I understood that the church of this monastery was considered as the most beautiful in Austria; and I can easily believe it to be so.

THROUGH THE TYROL*

BY WILLIAM CULLEN BRYANT

I left this most pleasing of the Italian cities (Venice), and took the road for the Tyrol. We

*From "Letters of a Traveller." The Tyrol and the Dolomites being mainly Austrian territory, are here included under "Other Austrian Scenes." Resorts in the Swiss Alps, including Chamouni (which, however, is in France), will be found further on in this volume.

passed through a level fertile country, formerly the territory of Venice, watered by the Piave, which ran blood in one of Bonaparte's battles. At evening we arrived at Ceneda, where our Italian poet Da Ponte* was born, situated just at the base of the Alps, the rocky peaks and irregular spires of which, beautifully green with the showery season, rose in the background. Ceneda seems to have something of German cleanliness about it, and the floors of a very comfortable inn at which we stopt were of wood, the first we had seen in Italy, tho common throughout Tyrol and the rest of Germany. A troop of barelegged boys, just broke loose from school, whooping and swinging their books and slates in the air, passed under my window.

On leaving Ceneda, we entered a pass in the mountains, the gorge of which was occupied by the ancient town of Serravalle, resting on arcades, the architecture of which denoted that it was built during the Middle Ages. Near it I remarked an old castle, which formerly commanded the pass, one of the finest ruins of the kind I had ever seen. It had a considerable extent of battlemented wall in perfect preservation, and both that and its circular tower were so luxuriantly loaded with ivy that they seemed almost to have been cut out of the living verdure. As we proceeded we became aware how worthy this region was to be the birthplace of a poet.

A rapid stream, a branch of the Piave, tinged of a light and somewhat turbid blue by the soil of

*An Italian poet (1749-1838), who, banished from Venice, settled in New York and became Professor of Italian at Columbia College.

OTHER AUSTRIAN SCENES

the mountains, came tumbling and roaring down the narrow valley; perpendicular precipices rose on each side; and beyond, the gigantic brotherhood of the Alps, in two long files of steep pointed summits, divided by deep ravines, stretched away in the sunshine to the northeast. In the face of one of the precipices by the way-side, a marble slab is fixt, informing the traveler that the road was opened by the late Emperor of Germany in the year of 1830. We followed this romantic valley for a considerable distance, passing several little blue lakes lying in their granite basins, one of which is called the "Lago Morto" or Dead Lake, from having no outlet for its waters.

At length we began to ascend, by a winding road, the steep sides of the Alps—the prospect enlarging as we went, the mountain summits rising to sight around us, one behind another, some of them white with snow, over which the wind blew with a wintry keenness—deep valleys opening below us, and gulfs yawning between rocks over which old bridges were thrown—and solemn fir forests clothing the broad declivities. The farm-houses placed on these heights, instead of being of brick or stone, as in the plains and valleys below, were principally built of wood; the second story, which served for a barn, being encircled by a long gallery, and covered with a projecting roof of plank held down with large stones.

We stopt at Venas, a wretched place with a wretched inn, the hostess of which showed us a chin swollen with the goitre, and ushered us into dirty comfortless rooms where we passed the night. When we awoke the rain was beating against the windows, and, on looking out, the forest and sides of the neighboring mountains, at a little height above us, appeared hoary with snow. We set out in the rain, but had not proceeded far before we heard the sleet striking against the windows of the carriage, and soon came to where the snow covered the ground to the depth of one or two inches.

Continuing to ascend, we passed out of Italy and entered the Tyrol. The storm had ceased before we went through the first Tyrolese village, and we could not help being struck with the change in the appearance of the inhabitants—the different costume, the less erect figures, the awkward gait, the lighter complexions, the neatly-kept inhabitations, and the absence of beggars. As we advanced, the clouds began to roll off from the landscape, disclosing here and there, through openings in their broad skirts as they swept along, glimpses of the profound valleys below us, and of the white sides and summits of mountains in the mid-sky above. At length the sun appeared, and revealed a prospect of such wildness, grandeur, and splendor as I have never before seen.

Lofty peaks of the most fantastic shapes, with deep clefts between, sharp needles of rock, and overhanging crags, infinite in multitude, shot up everywhere around us, glistening in the new-fallen snow, with thin wreaths of mist creeping along their sides. At intervals, swollen torrents, looking at a distance like long trains of foam, came thundering down the mountains, and crossing the road, plunged into the verdant valleys which winded beneath. Beside the highway were fields of young grain, prest to the ground with the snow; and in the meadows, ranunculuses of the size of roses, large yellow violets, and a thousand other Alpine

OTHER AUSTRIAN SCENES

flowers of the most brilliant hues, were peeping through their white covering.

We stopt to breakfast at a place called Landro, a solitary inn, in the midst of this grand scenery, with a little chapel beside it. The water from the dissolving snow was dropping merrily from the roof in a bright June sun. We needed not to be told that we were in Germany, for we saw it plainly enough in the nicely-washed floor of the apartment into which we were shown, in the neat cupboard with the old prayer-book lying upon it, and in the general appearance of housewifery; to say nothing of the evidence we had in the beer and tobacco-smoke of the travelers' room, and the guttural dialect and quiet tones of the guests.

From Landro we descended gradually into the beautiful valleys of the Tyrol, leaving the snow behind, tho the white peaks of the mountains were continually in sight. At Bruneck, in an inn resplendent with neatness—we had the first specimen of a German bed. It is narrow and short, and made so high at the head, by a number of huge square bolsters and pillows, that you rather sit than lie. The principal covering is a bag of down, very properly denominated the upper bed, and between this and the feather-bed below, the traveler is expected to pass a night. An asthmatic patient on a cold winter night might perhaps find such a couch tolerably comfortable, if he could prevent the narrow covering from slipping off on one side or the other.

The next day we were afforded an opportunity of observing more closely the inhabitants of this singular region, by a festival, or holiday of some

SEEING EUROPE WITH FAMOUS AUTHORS

sort, which brought them into the roads in great numbers, arrayed in their best dresses—the men in short jackets and small-clothes, with broad gay-colored suspenders over their waistcoats, and leathern belts ornamented with gold or silver leaf—the women in short petticoats composed of horizontal bands of different colors—and both sexes, for the most part, wearing broad-brimmed hats with hemispherical crowns, tho there was a sugar-loaf variety much affected by the men, adorned with a band of lace and sometimes a knot of flowers. They are a robust, healthy-looking race, tho they have an awkward stoop in the shoulders. But what struck me most forcibly was the devotional habits of the people.

The Tyrolese might be cited as an illustration of the remark, that mountaineers are more habitually and profoundly religious than others. Persons of all sexes, young and old, whom we meet in the road, were repeating their prayers audibly. We passed a troop of old women, all in broad-brimmed hats and short gray petticoats, carrying long staves, one of whom held a bead-roll and gave out the prayers, to which the others made the responses in chorus. They looked at us so solemnly from under their broad brims, and marched along with so grave and deliberate a pace, that I could hardly help fancying that the wicked Austrians had caught a dozen elders of the respectable Society of Friends, and put them in petticoats to punish them for their heresy. We afterward saw persons going to the labors of the day, or returning, telling their rosaries and saying their prayers as they went, as if their devotions had been their favorite amusement.

OTHER AUSTRIAN SCENES

At regular intervals of about half a mile, we saw wooden crucifixes erected by the way-side, covered from the weather with little sheds, bearing the image of the Savior, crowned with thorns and frightfully dashed with streaks and drops of red paint, to represent the blood that flowed from his wounds. The outer walls of the better kind of houses were ornamented with paintings in fresco, and the subjects of these were mostly sacred, such as the Virgin and Child, the Crucifixion, and the Ascension. The number of houses of worship was surprising; I do not mean spacious or stately churches such as we meet with in Italy, but most commonly little chapels dispersed so as best to accommodate the population. Of these the smallest neighborhood has one for the morning devotions of its inhabitants, and even the solitary inn has its little consecrated building with its miniature spire, for the convenience of pious wayfarers.

At Sterzing, a little village beautifully situated at the base of the mountain called the Brenner, and containing, as I should judge, not more than two or three thousand inhabitants, we counted seven churches and chapels within the compass of a square mile. The observances of the Roman Catholic church are nowhere more rigidly complied with than in the Tyrol. When we stopt at Bruneck on Friday evening, I happened to drop a word about a little meat for dinner in a conversation with the spruce-looking landlady, who appeared so shocked that I gave up the point, on the promise of some excellent and remarkably well-flavored trout from the stream that flowed through the village—a promise that was literally fulfilled. . . .

We descended the Brenner on the 28th of June

in a snow-storm, the wind whirling the light flakes in the air as it does with us in winter. It changed to rain, however, as we approached the beautiful and picturesque valley watered by the river Inn, on the banks of which stands the fine old town of Innsbruck, the capital of the Tyrol. Here we visited the Church of the Holy Cross, in which is the bronze tomb of Maxmilian I. and twenty or thirty bronze statues ranged on each side of the nave, representing fierce warrior-chiefs, and gowned prelates, and stately damsels of the middle ages. These are all curious for the costume; the warriors are cased in various kinds of ancient armor, and brandish various ancient weapons, and the robes of the females are flowing and by no means ungraceful. Almost every one of the statues has its hands and fingers in some constrained and awkward position; as if the artist knew as little what to do with them as some awkward and bashful people know what to do with their own. Such a crowd of figures in that ancient garb, occupying the floor in the midst of the living worshipers of the present day, has an effect which at first is startling.

From Innsbruck we climbed and crossed another mountain-ridge, scarcely less wild and majestic in its scenery than those we had left behind. On descending, we observed that the crucifixes had disappeared from the roads, and the broad-brimmed and sugar-loaf hats from the heads of the peasantry; the men wore hats contracted in the middle of the crown like an hour-glass, and the women caps edged with a broad band of black fur, the frescoes on the outside of the houses became less frequent; in short it was apparent that we had entered a different region, even if the custom-house and police officers on the frontier had not signified to us that we were now in the kingdom of Bavaria. We passed through extensive forests of fir, here and there checkered with farms, and finally came to the broad elevated plain bathed by the Isar, in which Munich is situated.

IN THE DOLOMITES*

BY ARCHIBALD CAMPBELL KNOWLES

The Dolomites are part of the Southern Tyrol. One portion is Italian, one portion is Austrian, and the rivalry of the two nations is keen. Under a warm summer sun, the quaint little villages seem half asleep, and the inhabitants appear to drift dreamily through life. Yet this is more apparent than real for, in many respects, the people here are busy in their own way.

Crossing this region are many mountain ranges of limestone structure, which by water, weather and other causes have been worn away into the most fantastic fissures and clefts and the most picturesque peaks and pinnacles. A very great charm is their curious coloring, often of great beauty. The region of the Dolomites is a great contrast to the rest of the Alps. Its characteristics do not make the same appeal to all. This is largely not only a matter of individual taste and temperament but also of one's mental or spiritual constitution, for the picture with its setting depends as much upon what it suggests as upon its con-

*From "Adventures in the Alps." Published by George W. Jacobs & Co.

stituent parts. The Dolomites suggest Italy in the contour of the country, in the grace of the inhabitants and in the colors which make the scene one of rich magnificence. The great artist Titian was born here* and he probably learned much from his observation of his native place.

Many of the mountain ranges are of the usual gray but such is the atmospheric condition that they seem to reflect the rosy rays of the setting sun or the purplish haze that often is found. The peaks are not great peaks in the sense that we speak of Mont Blanc, the Jungfrau, the Matterhorn or Monte Rosa. They impress one more as pictures with wonderful lights and strange grouping. . . .

If the reader intends some day to visit the Dolomites he is advised to enter from the north. Salzburg and the Salzkammergut, so much frequented by the Emperor Francis Joseph and the Austrian nobility, make a good introduction. Then by way of Innsbruck, one of the gems of the Tyrol, Toblach is reached, where the driving tour may properly begin. Toblach is a lovely place, if one stops long enough to see it and enjoy it! It is not very far to Cortina, the center of this beautiful region. The way there is very lovely. And driving is in keeping with the spirit of the place. It almost seems profane to rush through in a motor, as some do, for not only is it impossible to appreciate the scenery, but also it is out of harmony with the peace and quiet which reign.

For a while there is traversed a little valley quite embowered in green, but presently this

*In the village of Cadore—hence the name, Titian da Cadore.

OTHER AUSTRIAN SCENES

abruptly leads into a wild gorge, with jagged peaks on every side. Soon Monte Cristallo appears. This is the most striking of all the Dolomite peaks. At a tiny village, called Schluderbach, the road forks, that to the right going directly to Cortina, the other to the left proceeding by way of Lake Misurina. Lake Misurina is a pretty stretch of water, pale green in color and at an altitude of about 5,800 feet. On its shores are two very attractive and well-kept hotels, with charming walks, from which one looks on a splendid panorama, picturesque in extreme.

From Misurina, the road again ascends, becoming very narrow and very steep. The top is called "Passo Tre Croci," the Pass of the Three Crosses. The outlook is very lovely, with the three serrated peaks Monte Cristallo, Monte Piano and Monte Tofana, standing as guardian sentinels over the little valley of Ampezzo far below, where lies Cortina sleeping in the sun, while in the distance shine the snow fields of the Marmolata. Just as steeply as it climbed up one side, the road descends on the other side, to Cortina. This place is the capital of the valley and altogether lovely; beautiful in its woods and meadows, beautiful in its mountain views, beautiful in the town itself and beautiful in its people.

Cortina has much to boast of—an ancient church and some old houses; an industrial school in which the villagers are taught the most delicate and artistic (and withal comparatively cheap) filigree mosaic work; and a community of people, handsome in face and figure and possessing a carriage and refinement superior to any seen elsewhere among the mountaineers or peasantry. In the neighborhood of Cortina are many excursions and also extended rock climbs, but those who go there in the summer will be more apt to linger lazily amid the cool shade of the trees than to brave the hot Italian sun on the peaks!

After a few days' stay at Cortina, the drive is continued. There are many ways out. You can return by a new route to Toblach and the Upper Tyrol. Or you can go south to Belluno and thence to northern Italy. Or a third way and perhaps the finest tour of all is that over a series of magnificent mountain passes to Botzen. This last crosses the Ampezzo Valley and then begins the ascent of Monte Tofana, which here is beautifully wooded. Steepness seems characteristic of this region!

It is hard to imagine a carriage climbing a road any steeper than that one on the slopes of Monte Tofana! If narrow and steep is the way and hard and toilsome the climb this Monte Tofana route most certainly repays one when it reaches the Falzarego Pass (6,945 feet high) which is certainly an earthly Paradise! One can not aptly describe a view like that! It is all a picture; as if every part was purposely what it is, here rocky, here green, here snowy, with summits, valleys, ravines and villages and even a partly ruined castle to form a whole such as an artist or poet would revel in.

After a pause on the summit of the Pass, again comes a steep descent, as the drive is resumed, which continues to Andraz, where déjeuner is taken. One can not live on air or scenery and even the most indefatigable sightseer sometimes turns with longing to luncheon! Then one returns with added

OTHER AUSTRIAN SCENES

zest to the feast of eye and soul. And at Andraz, as one lingers awhile after luncheon on that high mountain terrace, a lovelier scene than that spread before the eye could scarcely be imagined. Indeed it is a "dream-scene," and as seen in the sleepy stillness of the early afternoon, when the shadows are already playing with the lights and gradually overcoming them, it seems like fancy, not reality.

Again the carriage is taken and soon the road is climbing once more, this time giving fine views of the Sella group of peaks and going through a series of picturesque valleys. At Arabba (5,255 feet), a pretty little village, the final ascent to Pordoi begins. The scenery undergoes a change. It becomes more wild and barren and the characteristics of the high Alps appear. The hour begins to be late and it becomes cold, but the light still lingers as the carriage reaches the summit of the pass and stops at the new Hôtel Pordoi (7,020 feet high) facing the weird, fantastic shapes of the Rosengarten and the Langkofel, on the one side and on the other the snowy Marmolata and the summits about Cortina. . . .

The following morning the start is made for Botzen. The way steadily descends for hours, past the pretty hamlets of Canazei, Campitello and Vigo di Fassa, surrounded by an imposing array of Dolomite peaks. After crossing the Karer Pass the scenery becomes much more soft and pastoral. Below the pass, most beautifully situated is a little green lake called the Karer-See. . . .

At Botzen the drive through the Dolomites ends. At best it gives but a glimpse of this delightful region! That glimpse leaves a lasting impression, not of snowy summits and glistening glaciers, but of wonderful rocks and more wonderful coloring and of great peaks of fantastic form, set in a garden spot of green. And Botzen is a fitting terminus. It dates far back to the Middle Ages. It boasts of churches, houses and public buildings of artistic merit and architectural beauty and over all there lingers an atmosphere of rest and refinement, refreshing to see, where there might have been the noisy bustle and hopeless vulgarity of so many places similarly situated.

There is plenty going on, nevertheless, for Botzen is quite a little commercial center in its own way, but with it there is this charm of dignified repose. One wanders through the town under the cool colonnades, strolls into some ancient cloisters, kneels for a moment in some finely carved church and then goes out again to the open, to see far above the little city that beautiful background of the Dolomite peaks, dominated by the wonderfully impressive and fantastic Rosengarten range, golden red in the western sun. With such a view experience may well lapse into memory, to linger on so long as the mind possesses the power of recalling the past.

OTHER AUSTRIAN SCENES

CORTINA*

BY AMELIA B. EDWARDS

Situate on the left bank of the Boita, which here runs nearly due north and south, with the Tre Croci pass opening away behind the town to the east, and the Tre Sassi Pass widening before it to the west, Cortina lies in a comparatively open space between four great mountains, and is therefore less liable to danger from bergfalls than any other village not only in the Val d'Ampezo but in the whole adjacent district. For the same reason, it is cooler in summer than either Caprile, Agordo, Primiero, or Predazzo; all of which, tho more central as stopping places, and in many respects more convenient, are yet somewhat too closely hemmed in by surrounding heights. The climate of Cortina is temperate throughout the year. Ball gives the village an elevation of 4,048 feet above the level of the sea; and one of the parish priests —an intelligent old man who has devoted many years of his life to collecting the flora of the Ampezzo—assured me that he had never known the thermometer drop so low as fifteen degrees† of frost in even the coldest winters. The soil, for all this, has a bleak and barren look; the maize (here called "grano Turco") is cultivated, but does not flourish; and the vine is unknown. But then agriculture is not a specialty of the Ampezzo Thal, and the wealth of Cortina is derived

*From "Untrodden Peaks and Unfrequented Valleys: A Midsummer Ramble in the Dolomites." Published by E. P. Dutton & Co.

†Reaumur.—Author's note.

essentially from its pasture-lands and forests.

These last, in consequence of the increased and increasing value of timber, have been lavishly cut down of late years by the Commune—too probably at the expense of the future interests of Cortina. For the present, however, every inn, homestead, and public building bespeaks prosperity. The inhabitants are well-fed and well-drest. Their fairs and festivals are the most considerable in all the South Eastern Tyrol; their principal church is the largest this side of St. Ulrich; and their new Gothic Campanile, 250 feet high, might suitably adorn the piazza of such cities as Bergamo or Belluno.

The village contains about 700 souls, but the population of the Commune numbers over 2,500. Of these, the greater part, old and young, rich and poor, men, women, and children, are engaged in the timber trade. Some cut the wood; some transport it. The wealthy convey it on trucks drawn by fine horses which, however, are cruelly overworked. The poor harness themselves six or eight in a team, men, women, and boys together, and so, under the burning summer sun, drag loads that look as if they might be too much for an elephant. . . .

To ascend the Campanile and get the near view over the village, was obviously one of the first duties of a visitor; so, finding the door open and the old bellringer inside, we mounted laboriously to the top—nearly a hundred feet higher than the Leaning Tower of Pisa. Standing here upon the outer gallery above the level of the great bells, we had the village and valley at our feet. The panorama, tho it included little which we had not

OTHER AUSTRIAN SCENES

seen already, was fine all around, and served to impress the mainland marks upon our memory. The Ampezzo Thal opened away to north and south, and the twin passes of the Tre Croci and Tre Sassi intersected it to east and west. When we had fixt in our minds the fact that Landro and Bruneck lay out to the north, and Perarolo to the south; that Auronzo was to be found somewhere on the other side of the Tre Croci; and that to arrive at Caprile it was necessary to go over the Tre Sassi, we had gained something in the way of definite topograhy. The Marmolata and Civetta, as we knew by our maps, were on the side of Caprile; and the Marmarole on the side of Auronzo. The Pelmo, left behind yesterday, was peeping even now above the ridge of the Rochetta; and a group of fantastic rocks, so like the towers and bastions of a ruined castle that we took them at first sight for the remains of some medieval stronghold, marked the summit of the Tre Sassi to the west.

"But what mountain is that far away to the south?" we asked, pointing in the direction of Perarolo.

"Which mountain, Signora?"

"That one yonder, like a cathedral front with two towers."

The old bellringer shaded his eyes with one trembling hand, and peered down the valley.

"Eh," he said, "it is some mountain on the Italian side."

"But what is it called?"

"Eh," he repeated, with a puzzled look, "who knows? I don't know that I ever noticed it before."

Now it was a very singular mountain—one of

the most singular and the most striking that we saw throughout the tour. It was exactly like the front of Notre Dame, with one slender aiguille, like a flagstaff, shooting up from the top of one of its battlemented towers. It was conspicuous from most points on the left bank of the Boita; but the best view, as I soon after discovered, was from the rising ground behind Cortina, going up through the fields in the direction of the Begontina torrent.

To this spot we returned again and again, fascinated as much, perhaps, by the mystery in which it was enveloped, as by the majestic outline of this unknown mountain, to which, for want of a better, we gave the name of Notre Dame. For the old bellringer was not alone in his ignorance. Ask whom we would, we invariably received the same vague reply—it was a mountain "on the Italian side." They knew no more; and some, like our friend of the Campanile, had evidently "not noticed it before."

IX

ALPINE RESORTS

THE CALL OF THE MOUNTAINS*

BY FREDERIC HARRISON

Once more—perhaps for the last time—I listen to the unnumbered tinkling of the cow-bells on the slopes—"the sweet bells of the sauntering herd"—to the music of the cicadas in the sunshine, and the shouts of the neat herdlads, echoing back from Alp to Alp. I hear the bubbling of the mountain rill, I watch the emerald moss of the pastures gleaming in the light, and now and then the soft white mist creeping along the glen, as our poet says, "puts forth an arm and creeps from pine to pine." And see, the wild flowers, even in this waning season of the year, the delicate lilac of the dear autumn crocus, which seems to start up elf-like out of the lush grass, the coral beads of the rowan, and the beech-trees just begun to wear their autumn jewelry of old gold.

As I stroll about these hills, more leisurely, more thoughtfully than I used to do of old in my hot mountaineering days, I have tried to think out what it is that makes the Alpine landscape so marvelous a tonic to the spirit—what is the special charm of it to those who have once felt all its inexhaustible magic. Other lands have rare beau-

*From "My Alpine Jubilee." Published in 1908.

ties, wonders of their own, sights to live in the memory for ever.

In France, in Italy, in Spain, in Greece and in Turkey, I hold in memory many a superb landscape. From boyhood upward I thirsted for all kinds of Nature's gifts, whether by sea, or by river, lake, mountain, or forest. For sixty years at least I have roved about the white cliffs, the moors, the riversides, lakes, and pastures of our own islands from Penzance to Cape Wrath, from Beachy Head to the Shetlands. I love them all. But they can not touch me, as do the Alps, with the sense at once of inexhaustible loveliness and of a sort of conscious sympathy with every fiber of man's heart and brain. Why then is this so?

I find it in the immense range of the moods in which Nature is seen in the Alps, as least by those who have fully absorbed all the forms, sights, sounds, wonders, and adventures they offer. An hour's walk will show them all in profound contrast and yet in exquisite harmony. The Alps form a book of Nature as wide and as mysterious as Life.

Earth has no scenes of placid fruitfulness more balmy than the banks of one of the larger lakes, crowded with vineyards, orchards, groves and pastures, down to the edge of its watery mirror, wherein, beside a semi-tropical vegetation, we see the image of some medieval castle, of some historic tower, and thence the eye strays up to sunless gorges, swept with avalanches, and steaming with feathery cascades; and higher yet one sees against the skyline ranges of terrific crags, girt with glaciers, and so often wreathed in storm clouds.

All that Earth has of most sweet, softest, easiest, most suggestive of langor and love, of fertility and abundance—here is seen in one vision beside all that Nature has most hard, most cruel, most unkind to Man—where life is one long weary battle with a frost bitten soil, and every peasant's hut has been built up stone by stone, and log by log, with sweat and groans, and wrecked hopes. In a few hours one may pass from an enchanted garden, where every sense is satiated, and every flower and leaf and gleam of light is intoxication, up into a wilderness of difficult crags and yawning glaciers, which men can reach only by hard-earned skill, tough muscle and iron nerves. . . .

The Alps are international, European, Humanitarian. Four written languages are spoken in their valleys, and ten times as many local dialects. The Alps are not especially Swiss—I used to think they were English—they belong equally to four nations of Europe; they are the sanatorium and the diversorium of the civilized world, the refuge, the asylum, the second home of men and women famous throughout the centuries for arts, literature, thought, religion. The poet, the philosopher, the dreamer, the patriot, the exile, the bereaved, the reformer, the prophet, the hero—have all found in the Alps a haven of rest, a new home where the wicked cease from troubling, where men need neither fear nor suffer. The happy and the thoughtless, the thinker and the sick—are alike at home here. The patriot exile inscribed on his house on Lake Leman—"Every land is fatherland to the brave man." What he might have written is—"This land is fatherland to all men." To young and old, to strong and weak, to wise and foolish alike, the Alps are a second fatherland.

INTERLAKEN AND THE JUNGFRAU*

BY ARCHIBALD CAMPBELL KNOWLES

It is hard to find a prettier spot than Interlaken. Situated between two lovely lakes, surrounded by wooded heights, and lying but a few miles from the snowy Jungfrau, it is like a jewel richly set. From Lucerne over the Brunig, from Meiringen over the Grimsel come the travelers, passing on their way the Lake of Brienz, with the waterfall of the Giessbach, on its southern side.

From Berne over Lake Thun, from the Rhône Valley over the Gemmi or through the Simmenthal come the tourists, seeing as they come the white peaks of the Oberland. And Interlaken welcomes them all, and rests them for their closer relations with the High Alps by trips to the region of the Lauterbrunnen, Grindelwald, and Mürren, and the great mountain plateaux looking down upon them. Interlaken is not a climbing center. Consequently mountaineering is little in evidence, conversation about ascents is seldom heard, and ice-axes, ropes, and nailed boots are seen more often in shop windows than in the streets.

Interlaken is not like some other Swiss towns. Berne, Geneva, Zurich, and Lucerne are places possessing notable churches, museums, and monuments of the past, having a social life of their own and being distinguished in some special way, as centers of culture and education. Interlaken, however, has little life apart from that made by the throngs of visitors who gather here in the

*From "Adventures in the Alps." Published by George W. Jacobs Company, Philadelphia.

ALPINE RESORTS

summer. There is little to see except a group of old monastic buildings, and in Unterseen and elsewhere some fine old carved chalets, but none of these receives much attention.

The attraction, on what one may call the natural side, centers in the softly beautiful panorama of woods and meadows, green hills and snow peaks which opens to the eye, and on the social side in the busy little promenade and park of the Höheweg, bordered with hotels, shops, and gardens. Here is ever a changing picture in the height of the season, in fact, quite kaleidoscopic as railways and steamboats at each end of Interlaken send their passengers to mingle in the passing crowd. All "sorts and conditions of men" are here, and representatives of antagonistic nations meet in friendly intercourse.

On the hotel terraces and in the little cafés and tea rooms, one hears a babel of voices, every nation of Europe seeming to speak in its own native tongue. Life goes easily. There is a gaiety in the little town that is infectious. It is a sort of busy idleness. "To trip or not to trip" is the question. If the affirmative, then a rush to the mountain trains and comfortable cabs. If the negative, then a turning to the shops, where pretty things worthy of Paris or London are seen side by side with Swiss carvings and Swiss embroidery and many little superficial souvenirs. As the contents of the shops are exhibited in the windows, so the character of the visitors is shown by the crowds, and the life of the place is seen in the constant ebb and flow of the people on the Höheweg.

Interlaken is undoubtedly a tourist center, for

few trips to Switzerland overlook or omit this delightful spot. Thousands come here, who never go any nearer the High Alps. They are quite content to sit on the benches of the Höheweg, listening to the music and enjoying the view. There is a casino, most artistically planned, with plashing fountains, shady paths, and wonderful flowerbeds. Here many persons pass the day, and, contrary to what one might expect, it is quiet and restful, lounging in that parklike garden.

For, notwithstanding "the madding crowd," Interlaken is a little gem of a mountain town, with an undertone of repose and nobility, as if the spirit of the Alps asserted herself, reigning, as one might say, for all not ruling. And always smiling at the people, as it were, is the majestic Jungfrau, ever seeming close at hand, altho eight miles away. . . .

The pleasures of this little Swiss resort are exhaustless. The wooded hills of the Rugen give innumerable walks amid beautiful forests, with all their wealth of pine and larch and hardwood, their moss-clad rocks and waving ferns. In that pleasant shade hours may be passed close to nature. The lakes not only offer delightful water trips, but also charming excursions along the wooded shores, sometimes high above the lakes, giving varying views of great beauty. While, ever as with beckoning fingers, the great peaks, snow-capped or rock-summitted, call one across the verdant meadows into the higher valleys of Kienthal, Lauterbrunnen, Grindelwald, and Kandersteg, to the terraced heights above or up amid the great wild passes.

Interlaken is, above all, a garden of green. Perhaps the unusual amount of rain which falls to the

ALPINE RESORTS

lot of this valley accounts for its verdure. In any event, park, woods, meadow, garden, even the mountain sides are green, a vari-colored green, and interspersed with an abundance of flowers. Nowhere is the eye offended by anything inartistic or unpicturesque, but, on the contrary, the charm is so comprehensive that the visitor looks from place to place, from this bit to that bit, and ever sees new beauty.

To complete all, to accentuate in the minds of some this impression of green, is the majestic Jungfrau. Other views may be grander and more magnificent, but no view of the Jungfrau can compare in loveliness to that from Interlaken. A great white glistening mass, far up above green meadows, green forests, and green mountains, rises this peak, a shining summit of white. Fitly named the Virgin, the Jungfrau gives her benediction to Interlaken, serenely smiling at the valley and at the town lying so quietly at her feet—the Jungfrau crowned with snow, Interlaken drest in green!

In the golden glory of the sun, in the silver shimmer of the moon, the Jungfrau beckons, the Jungfrau calls! "Come," she seems to say, "come nearer! Come up to the heights! Come close to the running waters! Come." And that invitation falls on no unwilling ears, but in to the Grindelwald and to the Lauterbrunnen and up to Mürren go those who love the majestic Jungfrau! What a wonderful trip this is! It may shatter some ideals in being taken to such a height in a railway train, but even against one's convictions as to the proper way of seeing a mountain, when all has been said, the fact remains that this trip is wonderful beyond words. There is a strangeness in taking a train which leaves a garden of green in the early morning and in a few hours later, after valley and pass and tunnel, puts one out on snow fields over 11,000 feet above the sea, where are seen vast stretches of white, almost level with the summit of the Jungfrau close at hand, and below, stretching for miles, on the one side the great Aletsch Glacier, and on the other side the green valleys enclosed by the everlasting hills!

The route is by way of Lauterbrunnen, Wengen, and the Scheidegg, and after skirting the Eiger Glacier going by tunnel into the very bowels of the mountain. At Eigerwand, Rotstock, and Eismeer are stations, great galleries blasted out of the rock, with corridors leading to openings from which one has marvelous views.* Eismeer looks directly upon the huge sea of snow and ice, with immense masses of dazzling white so close as to make one reel with awe and astonishment. In fact, this view is really oppressive in its wild magnificence, so near and so grand is it. The Jungfraujoch is different. One is out in the open, so to speak; one walks over that vast plateau of snow over 11,000 feet high in the glorious sunlight, above most of the nearer peaks and looking down at a beautiful panorama. On one side of this plateau is the Jungfrau, on the other the Mönch, either of which can be climbed from here in about three hours.

Yet the eye lingers longer in the direction of the Aletsch Glacier than anywhere else, this frozen river running for miles and turning to the right at the little green basin of water full of pieces of floating ice, called the Marjelen Lake, or See, at

*Since the above was written, the railway has been extended up the Jungfrau itself.

ALPINE RESORTS

the foot of the Eggishorn, which is unique and lovely. Long ago it was formed in this corner of the glacier, and its blue waters are really melted snow, over which float icebergs shining in the sun. In such a position the lake underlaps the glacier for quite a distance, forming a low vaulted cavern in the ice. Every now and then one of these little bergs overbalances itself and turns over, the upper side then being a deep blue, and the lower side, which was formerly above, being a pure white.

Again turning toward the green valleys, one with the eye of an artist, who can perceive and differentiate varying shades of color, can not but admit that the Bernese Oberland is "par excellence" first. Even south of the Alps the verdure does not excel or even equal that to be seen here. There is something incomparably lovely about the Oberland valleys. It is indescribable, indefinable, for when one has exhausted the most extravagant terms of description, he feels that he has failed to picture the scene as he desired. Yet if one word should be chosen to convey the impression which the Oberland makes, the word would be "color." For whether one regards the snow summits as setting off the valleys, or the green meadows as setting off the peaks, it matters not, for the secret of their beauty lies in the richness and variety of the exquisite coloring wherein many wonderful shades of green predominate.

THE ALTDORF OF WILLIAM TELL*

BY W. D. M'CRACKAN

Let it be said at once that, altho the name of Altdorf is indissolubly linked with that of William Tell, the place arouses an interest which does not at all depend upon its associations with the famous archer. From the very first it gives one the impression of possessing a distinct personality, of ringing, as it were, to a note never heard before, and thus challenging attention to its peculiarities.

As you approach Altdorf from Flüelen, on the Lake of Lucerne, by the long white road, the first houses you reach are large structures of the conventional village type, plain, but evidently the homes of well-to-do people, and some even adorned with family coats-of-arms. In fact, this street is dedicated to the aristocracy, and formerly went by the name of the Herrengasse, the "Lane of the Lords." Beyond these fashionable houses is an open square, upon which faces a cosy inn—named, of course, after William Tell; and off on one side the large parish church, built in cheap baroco style, but containing a few objects of interest. . . .

There is a good deal of sight-seeing to be done in Altdorf, for so small a place. In the town hall are shown the tattered flags carried by the warriors of Uri in the early battles of the Confederation, the mace and sword of state which are borne by the beadles to the Landsgemeinde. In a somewhat inaccessible corner, a few houses off, the beginnings

*From "Teutonic Switzerland." By special arrangement with, and by permission of, the publishers, L. C. Page & Co. Copyright, 1894.

of a museum have been made. Here is another portrait of interest—that of the giant Püntener, a mercenary whose valor made him the terror of the enemy in the battle of Marignano, in 1515; so that when he was finally killed, they avenged themselves, according to a writing beneath the picture, by using his fat to smear their weapons, and by feeding their horses with oats from his carcass. Just outside the village stands the arsenal, whence, they say, old armor was taken and turned into shovels, when the St. Gothard Railroad was building, so poor and ignorant were the people.

If you are of the sterner sex, you can also penetrate into the Capuchin Monastery, and enter the gardens, where the terraces that rise behind the buildings are almost Italian in appearance, festooned with vines and radiant with roses. Not that the fame of this institution rests on such trivial matters, however. The brothers boast of two things: theirs is the oldest branch of the order in Switzerland, dating from 1581, and they carry on in it the somewhat unappetizing industry of cultivating snails for the gourmands of foreign countries. Above the Capuchins is the famous Bannwald, mentioned by Schiller—a tract of forest on the mountain-slope, in which no one is allowed to fell trees, because it protects the village from avalanches and rolling stones.

Nothing could be fairer than the outskirts of Altdorf on a May morning. The valley of the Reuss lies bathed from end to end in a flood of golden light, shining through an atmosphere of crystal purity. Daisies, cowslips, and buttercups, the flowers of rural well-being, show through the rising grass of the fields; along the hedges and crumbling walls of the lanes peep timid primroses and violets, and in wilder spots the Alpine gentian, intensely blue. High up, upon the mountains, glows the indescribable velvet of the slopes, while, higher still, ragged and vanishing patches of snow proclaim the rapid approach of summer.

After all, the best part of Altdorf, to make an Irish bull, lies outside of the village. No adequate idea of this strange little community can be given without referring to the Almend, or village common. Indeed, as time goes on, one learns to regard this Almend as the complete expression and final summing up of all that is best in Altdorf, the reconciliation of all its inconsistencies.

How fine that great pasture beside the River Reus, with its short, juicy, Alpine grass, in sight of the snow-capped Bristenstock, at one end of the valley, and of the waters of Lake Lucerne at the other! In May, the full-grown cattle have already departed for the higher summer pastures, leaving only the feeble young behind, who are to follow as soon as they have grown strong enough to bear the fatigues of the journey. At this time, therefore, the Almend becomes a sort of vision of youth—of calves, lambs, and foals, guarded by little boys, all gamboling in the exuberance of early life.

ALPINE RESORTS

LUCERNE*

BY VICTOR TISSOT

A height crowned with embattled ramparts that bristle with loop-holed turrets; church towers mingling their graceful spires and peaceful crosses with those warlike edifices; dazzling white villas, planted like tents under curtains of verdure; tall houses with old red skylights on the roofs—this is our first glimpse of the Catholic and warlike city of Lucerne. We seem to be approaching some town of old feudal times that has been left solitary and forgotten on the mountain side, outside of the current of modern life.

But when we pass through the station we find ourselves suddenly transported to the side of the lake, where whole flotillas of large and small boats lie moored on the blue waters of a large harbor. And along the banks of this wonderful lake is a whole town of hotels, gay with many colored flags, their terraces and balconies rising tier above tier, like the galleries of a grand theater whose scenery is the mighty Alps. . . .

In summer Lucerne is the Hyde Park of Switzerland. Its quays are thronged by people of every nation. There you meet pale women from the lands of snow, and dark women from the lands of the sun; tall, six-foot English women, and lively, alert, trim Parisian women, with the light and graceful carriage of a bird on the bough. At certain hours this promenade on the quays is like a

---

*From "Unknown Switzerland." Published by James Pott & Co.

charity fair or a rustic ball—bright colors and airy draperies everywhere.

Nowhere can the least calm and repose be found but in the old town. There the gabled houses, with wooden galleries hanging over the waters of the Reuss, make a charming ancient picture, like a bit of Venice set down amid the verdant landscape of the valley.

I also discovered on the heights beyond the ramparts a pretty and peaceful convent of Capuchins, the way to which winds among wild plants, starry with flowers. It is delicious to go right away, far from the town swarming and running over with Londoners, Germans, and Americans, and to find yourself among fragrant hedges, peopled by warblers whom it has not yet occurred to the hotel-keepers to teach to sing in English. This sweet path leads without fatigue to the convent of the good fathers.

In a garden flooded with sunshine and balmy with the fragrance of mignonette and vervain, where broad sunflowers erect their black discs fringed with gold, two brothers with fan-shaped beards, their brass-mounted spectacles astride on their flat noses, and arrayed in green gardening aprons, are plying enormous watering-cans; while, in the green and cool half-twilight under the shadowy trees, big, rubicund brothers walk up and down, reading their red-edged breviaries in black leather bindings.

Happy monks! Not a fraction of a pessimist among them! How well they understand life! A beautiful convent, beautiful nature, good wine and good cheer, neither disturbance nor care; neither wife nor children; and when they leave the

ALPINE RESORTS

world, heaven specially created for them, seraphim waiting for them with harps of gold, and angels with urns of rose-water to wash their feet!

Lucerne began as a nest of monks, hidden in an orchard like a nest of sparrows. The first house of the town was a monastery, erected by the side of the lake. The nest grew, became a village, then a town, then a city. The monks of Murbach, to whom the monastery of St. Leger belonged, had got into debt; this sometimes does happen even to monks. They sold to King Rudolf all the property they possest at Lucerne and in Unterwalden; and thus the town passed into the hands of the Hapsburgs.

When the first Cantons, after expelling the Austrian bailiffs, had declared their independence, Lucerne was still one of Austria's advanced posts. But its people were daily brought into contact with the shepherds of the Forest Cantons, who came into the town to supply themselves with provisions; and they were not long in beginning to ask themselves if there was any reason why they should not be, as well as their neighbors, absolutely free. The position of the partizans of Austria soon became so precarious that they found it safe to leave the town. . . .

The opening of the St. Gothard Railway has given a new impulse to this cosmopolitan city, which has a great future before it. Already it has supplanted Interlaken in the estimation of the furbelowed, fashionable world—the women who come to Switzerland not to see but to be seen. Lucerne is now the chief summer station of the twenty-two Cantons. And yet it does not possess many objects of interest. There is the old bridge on the Reuss, with its ancient paintings; the Church of St. Leger, with its lateral altars and its Campo Santo, reminding us of Italian cemeteries; the museum at the Town Hall, with its fine collection of stained glass; the blood-stained standards from the Burgundian wars, and the flag in which noble old Gundolfingen, after charging his fellow-citizens never to elect their magistrates for more than a year, wrapt himself as in a shroud of glory to die in the fight; finally, there is the Lion of Lucerne; and that is all.

The most wonderful thing of all is that you are allowed to see this lion for nothing; for close beside it you are charged a franc for permission to cast an indifferent glance on some uninteresting excavations, which date, it is said, from the glacial period. We do not care if they do. . . .

The great quay of Lucerne is delightful; as good as the seashore at Dieppe or Trouville. Before you, limpid and blue, lies the lake, which from the character of its shores, at once stern and graceful, is the finest in Switzerland. In front rises the snow-clad peaks of Uri, to the left the Rigi, to the right the austere Pilatus, almost always wearing his high cap of clouds. This beautiful walk on the quay, long and shady like the avenue of a gentleman's park, is the daily resort, toward four o'clock, of all the foreigners who are crowded in the hotels or packed in the boarding-houses. Here are Russian and Polish counts with long mustaches, and pins set with false brilliants; Englishmen with fishes' or horses' heads; Englishwomen with the figures of angels or of giraffes; Parisian women, daintily attired, sprightly, and coquettish; American women, free in their bearing, and eccentric in their dress, and their men as stiff as the smoke-pipes of steamboats; German women, with languishing voices, drooping and pale like willow branches, fair-haired and blue-eyed, talking in the same breath of Goethe and the price of sausages, of the moon and their glass of beer, of stars and black radishes. And here and there are a few little Swiss girls, fresh and rosy as wood strawberries, smiling darlings like Dresden shepherdesses, dreaming of scenes of platonic love in a great garden adorned with the statue of William Tell or General Dufour.

ZURICH*

BY W. D. M'CRACKAN

If you arrive in Zurich after dark, and pass along the river-front, you will think yourself for a moment in Venice. The street lamps glow responsively across the dark Limmat, or trail their light from the bridges. In the uncertain darkness, the bare house walls of the farther side put on the dignity of palaces. There are unsuspected architectural glories in the Wasserkirche and the Rathhaus, as they stand partly in the water of the river. And if, at such times, one of the long, narrow barges of the place passes up stream, the illusion is complete; for, as the boat cuts at intervals through the glare of gaslight it looks for all the world like a gondola. . . .

Zurich need not rely upon any fancied resem-

*From "Teutonic Switzerland." By special arrangement with, and by permission of, the publishers, L. C. Page & Co. Copyright, 1894.

blance of this sort for a distinct charm of its own. The situation of the city is essentially beautiful, reminding one, in a general way, of that of Geneva, Lucerne, or Thun—at the outlet of a lake, and at the point of issue of a swift river. Approaching from the lakeside, the twin towers of the Grossmünster loom upon the light, capped by ugly rounded tops, like miters; upon the left, the simple spires of the Fraumünster and St. Peter's. A conglomeration of roofs denotes the city houses. On the water-front, extensive promenades stretch, crescent shaped, from end to end, cleverly laid out, tho as yet too new to quite fulfil their mission of beauty. Some large white buildings form the front line on the lake—notably the theater, and a few hotels and apartment houses. Finally, there where the River Limmat leaves the lake, a vista of bridges open into the heart of the city—a succession of arches and lines that invite inspection.

Like most progressive cities of Europe, Zurich has outgrown its feudal accouterments within the last fifty years. It has razed its walls, converted its bastions into playgrounds, and, pushing out on every side, has incorporated many neighboring villages, until to-day it contains more than ninety thousand inhabitants.* The pride of modern Zurich is the Bahnhof-strasse, a long street which leads from the railroad station to the lake. It is planted with trees, and counts as the one, and only boulevard of the city. Unfortunately, a good view of the distant snow mountains is very rare from the lake promenade, altho they appear with distinctness upon the photographs sold in the shops.

*The population in 1902 had risen to 152,000.

ALPINE RESORTS

Early every Saturday the peasant women come trooping in, with their vegetables, fruits, and flowers, to line the Bahnhof-strasse with carts and baskets. The ladies and kitchen-maids of the city come to buy; but by noon the market is over. In a jiffy, the street is swept as clean as a kitchen floor, and the women have turned their backs on Zurich. But the real center of attraction in Zurich will be found by the traveler in that quarter where stands the Grossmünster, the church of which Zwingli was incumbent for twelve years.

It may well be called the Wittenberg church of Switzerland. The present building dates from the eleventh and twelfth centuries; but tradition has it that the first minster was founded by Charlemagne. That ubiquitous emperor certainly manifested great interest in Zurich. He has been represented no less than three times in various parts of the building. About midway up one of the towers, his statue appears in a niche, where pigeons strut and prink their feathers, undisturbed. Charlemagne is sitting with a mighty two-edged sword upon his knees, and a gilded crown upon his head; but the figure is badly proportioned, and the statue is a good-natured, stumpy affair, that makes one smile rather than admire. The outside of the minster still shows traces of the image breakers of Zwingli's time, and yet the crumbling north portal remains beautiful, even in decay. As for the interior, it has an exceedingly bare and stript appearance; for, altho there is good, solid stonework in the walls, the whole has been washed a foolish, Philistine white. The Romanesque of the architectural is said to be of particular interest to connoisseurs, and the queer archaic capitals must certainly attract the notice even of ordinary tourists. . . .

It is also worth while to go to the Helmhaus, and examine the collection of lake-dwelling remains. In fact, there is a delightful little model of a lake-dwelling itself, and an appliance to show you how those primitive people could make holes in their stone implements, before they knew the use of metals. The ancient guild houses of Zurich are worth a special study. Take, for instance, that of the "Zimmerleute," or carpenter with its supporting arches and little peaked tower; or the so-called "Waag," with frescoed front; then the great wainscoated and paneled hall of the "schmieden" (smiths); and the rich Renaissance stonework of the "Maurer" (masons). These buildings, alas, with the decay of the system which produced them, have been obliged to put up big signs of Café Restaurant upon their historic façades, like so many vulgar, modern eating-houses.

The Rathhaus, or Town Hall, too, is charming. It stands, like the Wasserkirche, with one side in the water and the other against the quay. The style is a sort of reposeful Italian Renaissance, that is florid only in the best artistic sense. Nor must you miss the so-called "Rüden," nearby, for its sloping roof and painted walls give it a very captivating look of alert picturesqueness, and it contains a large collection of Pestalozzi souvenirs.

Zurich has more than one claim to the world's recognition; but no department of its active life, perhaps, merits such unstinted praise as its educational facilities. First and foremost, the University, with four faculties, modeled upon the German system, but retaining certain distinctive traits that are essentially Swiss—for instance, the broad and liberal treatment accorded to women students, who are admitted as freely as men, and receive the same instruction. A great number of Russian girls are always to be seen in Zurich, as at other Swiss universities, working unremittingly to acquire the degrees which they are denied at home. Not a few American women also have availed themselves of these facilities, especially for the study of medicine. . . .

Zürich is, at the present time, undoubtedly the most important commercial city in Switzerland, having distanced both Basel and Geneva in this direction. The manufacturing of silk, woolen, and linen fabrics has flourished here since the end of the thirteenth century. In modern times, however, cotton and machinery have been added as staple articles of manufacture. Much of the actual weaving is still done in outlying parts of the Canton, in the very cottages of the peasants, so that the click of the loom is heard from open windows in every village and hamlet.

But modern industrial processes are tending continually to drive the weavers from their homes into great centralized factories, and every year this inevitable change becomes more apparent. It is certainly remarkable that Zürich should succeed in turning out cheap and good machinery, when we remember that every ton of coal and iron has to be imported, since Switzerland possesses not a single mine, either of the one or the other.

THE RIGI*

BY W. D. M'CRACKAN

If you really want to know how the Swiss Confederation came to be, you can not do better than take the train to the top of the Rigi. You might stumble through many a volume, and not learn so thoroughly the essential causes of this national birth.

Of course, the eye rests first upon the phalanx of snow-crests to the south, then down upon the lake, lying outstretched like some wriggling monster, switching its tail, and finally off to the many places where early Swiss history was made. In point of fact, you are looking at quite a large slice of Switzerland. Victor Hugo seized the meaning of this view when he wrote: "It is a serious hour, and full of meditations, when one has Switzerland thus under the eyes." . . .

The physical features of a country have their counterparts in its political institutions. In Switzerland the great mountain ranges divide the territory into deep valleys, each of which naturally forms a political unit—the Commune. Here is a miniature world, concentrated into a small space, and representing the sum total of life to its inhabitants. Self-government becomes second nature under these conditions. A sort of patriarchal democracy is evolved: that is, certain men and certain families are apt to maintain themselves

---

*From "Teutonic Switzerland." By special arrangement with, and by permission of, the publishers, L. C. Page & Co. Copyright, 1894.

ALPINE RESORTS

at the head of public affairs, but with the consent and cooperation of the whole population.

There is hardly a spot associated with the rise of the Swiss Confederation whose position can not be determined from the Rigi. The two Tell's chapels; the Rütli; the villages of Schwiz, Altdorf, Brunnen, Beckenried, Stans, and Sarnen; the battlefields of Morgarten and Sempach; and on a clear day the ruined castle of Hapsburg itself, lie within a mighty circle at one's feet.

It was preordained that the three lands of Uri, Schwiz, and Unterwalden should unite for protection of common interests against the encroachment of a common enemy—the ambitious house of Hapsburg. The lake formed at once a bond and a highway between them. On the first day of August, 1291, more than six hundred years ago, a group of unpretentious patriots, ignored by the great world, signed a document which formed these lands into a loose Confederation. By this act they laid the foundation upon which the Swiss state was afterward reared. In their naïve, but prophetic, faith, the contracting parties called this agreement a perpetual pact; and they set forth, in the Latin, legal phraseology of the day, that, seeing the malice of the times, they found it necessary to take an oath to defend one another against outsiders, and to keep order within their boundaries; at the same time carefully stating that the object of the league was to maintain lawfully established conditions.

From small beginnings, the Confederation of Uri, Schwiz, and Unterwalden grew, by the addition of other communities, until it reached its present proportions, of twenty-two Cantons, in 1815. Lucerne was the first to join; then came Zurich,

Glarus, Zug, Bern, etc. The early Swiss did not set up a sovereign republic, in our acceptation of the word, either in internal or external policy. The class distinctions of the feudal age continued to exist; and they by no means disputed the supreme rule of the head of the German Empire over them, but rather gloried in the protection which this direct dependence afforded them against a multitude of intermediate, preying nobles.

CHAMOUNI—AN AVALANCHE*

BY PERCY BYSSHE SHELLEY

From Servoz three leagues remain to Chamouni —Mont Blanc was before us—the Alps, with their innumerable glaciers on high all around, closing in the complicated windings of the single vale— forests inexpressibly beautiful, but majestic in their beauty—intermingled beech and pine, and oak, overshadowed our road, or receded, while lawns of such vendure as I have never seen before occupied these openings, and gradually became darker in their recesses. Mont Blanc was before us, but it was covered with cloud; its base, furrowed with dreadful gaps, was seen above. Pinnacles of snow intolerably bright, part of the chain connected with Mont Blanc, shone through the clouds at intervals

*From "The Letters of Percy Bysshe Shelley." Politically, Chamouni is in France, but the aim here has been to bring into one volume all the more popular Alpine resorts. Articles on the Tyrol and the Dolomites will also be found in this volume—under "Other Austrian Scenes."

ALPINE RESORTS

on high. I never knew—I never imagined—what mountains were before.

The immensity of these aerial summits excited, when they suddenly burst upon the sight, a sentiment of ecstatic wonder, not unallied to madness. And, remember, this was all one scene, it all prest home to our regard and our imagination. Tho it embraced a vast extent of space, the snowy pyramids which shot into the bright blue sky seemed to overhang our path; the ravine, clothed with gigantic pines, and black with its depth below, so deep that the very roaring of the untameable Arve, which rolled through it, could not be heard above— all was as much our own, as if we had been the creators of such impressions in the minds of others as now occupied our own. Nature was the poet, whose harmony held our spirits more breathless than that of the divinest.

As we entered the valley of the Chamouni (which, in fact, may be considered as a continuation of those which we have followed from Bonneville and Cluses), clouds hung upon the mountains at the distance perhaps of 6,000 feet from the earth, but so as effectually to conceal not only Mont Blanc, but the other "aiguilles," as they call them here, attached and subordinate to it. We were traveling along the valley, when suddenly we heard a sound as the burst of smothered thunder rolling above; yet there was something in the sound that told us it could not be thunder. Our guide hastily pointed out to us a part of the mountain opposite, from whence the sound came. It was an avalanche. We saw the smoke of its path among the rocks, and continued to hear at intervals the bursting of its fall. It fell on the bed of a torrent, which it displaced, and presently we saw its tawny-colored waters also spread themselves over the ravine, which was their couch.

We did not, as we intended, visit the Glacier des Bossons to-day, altho it descends within a few minutes' walk of the road, wishing to survey it at least when unfatigued. We saw this glacier, which comes close to the fertile plain, as we passed. Its surface was broken into a thousand unaccountable figures; conical and pyramidical crystallizations, more than fifty feet in height, rise from its surface, and precipices of ice, of dazzling splendor, overhang the woods and meadows of the vale. This glacier winds upward from the valley, until it joins the masses of frost from which it was produced above, winding through its own ravine like a bright belt flung over the black region of pines.

There is more in all these scenes than mere magnitude of proportion; there is a majesty of outline; there is an awful grace in the very colors which invest these wonderful shapes—a charm which is peculiar to them, quite distinct even from the reality of their unutterable greatness.

ZERMATT*

BY ARCHIBALD CAMPBELL KNOWLES

Those who would reach the very heart of the Alps and look upon a scene of unparalleled grandeur must go into the Valais to Zermatt.

*From "Adventures in the Alps." Published by George W. Jacobs & Co.

PONTRESINA IN THE ENGADINE

ST. MORITZ IN THE ENGADINE

FRIBOURG

BERNE

VIVEY ON LAKE GENEVA

Courtesy Swiss Federal Railway

THE TURNHALLE IN ZURICH

INTERLAKEN

LUCERNE

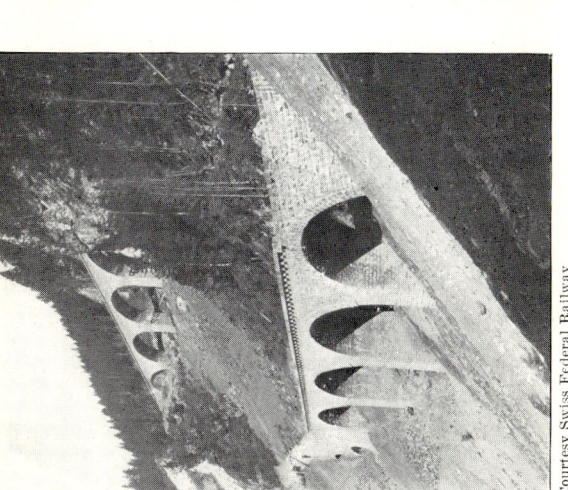

Courtesy Swiss Federal Railway
VIADUCTS
On the new Lötschberg route to the Simplon tunnel

Courtesy Swiss Federal Railway
WOLFORT VIADUCT
On the Pilatus Railroad, Switzerland

THE BALMAT-SAUSSURE MONUMENT IN CHAMONIX
(Mont Blanc in the distance)

ROOFED WOODEN BRIDGE AT LUCERNE

THE CASTLE OF CHILLON

Courtesy Swiss Federal Railway
CLOUD EFFECT ABOVE INTERLAKEN

Courtesy Swiss Federal Railway
DAVOS IN WINTER

ALPINE RESORTS

The way up the valley is that which follows the River Visp. It is a delightful journey. The little stream is never still. It will scarcely keep confined to the banks or within the stone walls which in many places protect the shores. The river dances along as if seeking to be free. For the most part it is a torrent, sweeping swiftly past the solid masonry and descending the steep bed in a series of wild leaps or artificial waterfalls, with wonderful effects of sunlight seen in the showers of spray. Fed as it is by many mountain streams, the Visp is always full, and the more so, when in summer the melting ice adds to its volume.

Then it is a sight long remembered, as roaring, rollicking, rushing along it is a brawling mass of waters, often working havoc with banks, road, village, and pastures. If one never saw a mountain, the sight of the Visp would more than repay, but, as it is, one's attention is taxed to the uttermost not to miss anything of this little rushing river and at the same time get the charming views of the Weisshorn, the Breithorn, and the other snow summits which appear over the mountain spurs surrounding the head of the valley.

The first impression on reaching the Zermatt is one of disappointment. Maps and pictures generally lead the traveler to think that from the village he will see the great semicircle of snow peaks which surround the valley, but upon arrival he finds that he must go further up to see them, for all of them are hidden from view except the Matterhorn.

This mountain, however, is seen in all its grandeur, fierce and frowning, and to an imaginative mind bending forward as if threatening and trying to shake off the little snow that appears here and there on its side. It dominates the whole scene and leaves an indelible impress on the mind, so that one can never picture Zermatt without the Matterhorn.

Zermatt as a place is a curious combination; a line of hotels in juxtaposition with a village of chalets, unsophisticated peasants shoulder to shoulder with people of fashion! There are funny little shops, here showing only such simple things as are needed by the dwellers in the Valais, there exhibiting really beautiful articles in dress and jewelry to attract the summer visitors, while at convenient spots are the inevitable tea-rooms, where "Thé, Café, Limonade, Confiserie" minister to the coming crowds of an afternoon. . . .

Guides galore wait in front of all the large hotels; ice-axes, ropes, nailed boots, rucksacks, and all the paraphernalia of the mountains are seen on every side, and a walk along the one main thoroughfare introduces one into the life of a climbing center, interesting to a degree and often very amusing from the miscellaneous collection of people there.

Perhaps the first thing one cares to see at Zermatt is the village church, with the adjoining churchyard. The church, dedicated to Saint Maurice, a favorite saint in the Valais and Rhône district, is plain but interesting and in parts is quite old. Near it is a little mortuary chapel. In most parts of Switzerland, it is the custom, after the bodies of the dead have been buried a certain length of time, to remove the remains to the "charnel house," allowing the graves to be used again and thus not encroaching upon the space

ALPINE RESORTS

reserved and consecrated in the churchyard, but we do not think this custom obtains at Zermatt.

In the churchyard is a monument to Michel Auguste Croz, the guide, and near by are the graves of the Reverend Charles Hudson and Mr. Hadow. These three, with Lord Francis Douglas were killed in Mr. Whymper's first ascent of the Matterhorn.* The body of Lord Francis Douglas has never been found. It is probably deep in some crevasse or under the snows which surround the base of the Matterhorn. . . .

For the more extended climbs or for excursions in the direction of the Schwarzsee, the Staffel Alp or the Trift, Zermatt is the starting point. The place abounds in walks, most of them being the first part of the routes to the high mountains, so that those who are fond of tramping but not of climbing can reach high elevations with a little hard work, but no great difficulty. Some of these "midway" places may be visited on muleback, and with the railway now up to the Gorner-Grat there are few persons who may not see this wonderful region of snow peaks.

The trip to the Schwarzsee is the first stage on the Matterhorn route. It leads through the village, past the Gorner Gorges (which one may visit by a slight détour) and then enters some very pretty woods, from which one issues on to the bare green meadows which clothe the upper part of the steep slope of the mountain. As one mounts this zigzag path, it sometimes seems as if it would never end, and for all the magnificent views

*For. Mr. Whymper's own account of this famous ascent, see page 127 of this volume.

SEEING EUROPE WITH FAMOUS AUTHORS

which it affords, one is always glad that it is over, as it exactly fulfils the conditions of a "grind."

From the Schwarzsee (8,495 feet, where there is an excellent hotel), there is a fine survey of the Matterhorn, and also a splendid panorama on three sides, one view up the glaciers toward the Monte Rosa, another over the valley to the Dent Blanche and other great peaks, and still another to the far distant Bernese Oberland. Near the hotel is a little lake and a tiny chapel, where mass is sometimes said. The reflection in the still waters of the lake is very lovely.

From the Schwarzsee, trips are made to the Hornli (another stage on the way to the Matterhorn), to the Gandegg Hut, across moraine and glacier and to the Staffel Alp, over the green meadows. The Hörnli (9,490 feet high) is the ridge running out from the Matterhorn. It is reached by a stiff climb over rocks and a huge heap of fallen stones and débris. From it the view is similar to that from the Schwarzsee, but much finer, the Théodule Glacier being seen to great advantage. Above the Hörnli towers the Matterhorn, huge, fierce, frowning, threatening. Every few moments comes a heavy, muffled sound, as new showers of falling stones come down. This is one of the main dangers in climbing the peak itself, for from base to summit, the Matterhorn is really a decaying mountain, the stones rolling away through the action of the storms, the frosts, and the sun.

ALPINE RESORTS

PONTRÉSINA AND ST. MORITZ*

BY VICTOR TISSOT

The night was falling fine as dust, as a black sifted snow-shower, a snow made of shadow; and the melancholy of the landscape, the grand nocturnal solitude of these lofty, unknown regions, had a charm profound and disquieting. I do not know why I fancied myself no longer in Switzerland, but in some country near the pole, in Sweden or Norway. At the foot of these bare mountains I looked for wild fjords, lit up by the moon.

Nothing can express the profound somberness of these landscapes at nightfall; the long desert road, gray from the reflections of the starry sky, unrolls in an interminable ribbon along the depth of the valley; the treeless mountains, hollowed out like ancient craters, lift their overhanging precipices; lakes sleeping in the midst of the pastures, behind curtains of pines and larches, glitter like drops of quicksilver; and on the horizon the immense glaciers crowd together and overflow like sheets of foam on a frozen sea.

The road ascends. From the distance comes a dull noise, the roaring of a torrent. We cross a little cluster of trees, and on issuing from it the superb amphitheater of glaciers shows itself anew, overlooked by one white point glittering like an opal. On the hill a thousand little lights show me that I am at last at Pontrésina. I thought I should never have arrived there; nowhere does night deceive more than in the mountains; in proportion

*From "Unknown Switzerland." Published by James Pott & Co.

as you advance toward a point, it seems to retreat from you.

Soon the black fantastic lines of the houses show through the darkness. I enter a narrow street, formed of great gloomy buildings, their fronts like a convent or prison. The hamlet is transformed into a little town of hotels, very comfortable, very elegant, very dear, but very stupid and very vulgar, with their laced porter in an admiral's hat, and their whiskered waiters, who have the air of Anglican ministers. Oh! how I detest them, and flee them, those hotels where the painter, or the tourist who arrives on foot, knapsack on his back and staff in hand, his trousers tucked into his leggings, his flask slung over his shoulder, and his hat awry, is received with less courtesy than a lackey.

Besides those hotels, some of which are veritable palaces, and where the ladies are almost bound to change their dress three times a day, there is a hotel of the second and third class; and there is the old inn; the comfortable, hospitable, patriarchal inn, with its Gothic signboard. . . .

On leaving the village I was again in the open mountain. In the distance the road penetrated into the valley, rising always. The moon had risen. She stood out sharply cut in a cloudless sky, and stars sparkling everywhere in profusion; not like nails of gold, but sown broadcast like a flying dust, a dust of carbuncles and diamonds. To the right, in the depths of the amphitheater of the mountains, an immense glacier looked like a frozen cascade; and above, a perfectly white peak rose draped in snow, like some legendary king in his mantle of silver.

ALPINE RESORTS

Bending under my knapsack, and dragging my feet, I arrive at last at the hotel, where I am received, in the kindest manner in the world, by the two mistresses of the establishment, two sisters of open, benevolent countenance and of sweet expression.

And the poor little traveler who arrives, his bag on his back and without bustle, who has sent neither letter nor telegram to announce his arrival, is the object of the kindest and most delicate attentions; his clothes are brushed, he gets water for his refreshment, and is then conducted to a table bountifully spread, in a dining-room fragrant with good cookery and bouquets of flowers. . . .

Beyond Campfer, its houses surrounding a third little lake, we come suddenly on a scene of extraordinary animation. All the cosmopolitan society of St. Moritz is there, sauntering, walking, running, in mountain parties, on afternoon excursions. The favorite one is the walk to the pretty lake of Campfer, with its shady margin, its resting places hidden among the branches, its châlet-restaurant, from the terrace of which one overlooks the whole valley; and it would be difficult to find near St. Moritz a more interesting spot.

We meet at every step parties of English ladies, looking like plantations of umbrellas with their covers on and surmounted by immense straw hats; then there are German ladies, massive as citadels, but not impregnable, asking nothing better than to surrender to the young exquisites, with the figure of cuirassiers, who accompany them; further on, lively Italian ladies parade themselves in dresses of the carnival, the colors outrageously striking and dazzling to the eyes; with up-turned skirts they cross the Inn on great mossy stones, leaping with the grace of birds, and smiling, to show, into the bargain, the whiteness of their teeth. All this crowd passing in procession before us is composed of men and women of every age and condition; some with the grave face of a waxen saint, others beaming with the satisfied smile of rich people; there are also invalids, who go along hobbling and limping, or who are drawn in little carriages.

Soon handsome façades, pierced with hundreds of windows, show themselves in the grand and severe setting of mountains and glaciers. It is St. Moritz-les-Bains. Here every house is a hotel, and, as every hotel is a little palace, we do not alight from the diligence; we go a little farther and a little higher, to St. Moritz-le-Village, which has a much more beautiful situation. It is at the top of a little hill, whose sides slope down to a pretty lake, fresh and green as a lawn. The eye reaches beyond Sils, the whole length of the valley, with its mountains like embattled ramparts, its lakes like a great w of pearls, and its glaciers showing their piles of snowy white against the azure depths of the horizon.

St. Moritz is the center of the valley of the Upper Engadine, which extends to the length of eighteen or nineteen leagues, and which scarcely possesses a thousand inhabitants. Almost all the men emigrate to work for strangers, like their brothers, the mountaineers of Savoy and Auvergne, and do not return till they have amassed a sufficient fortune to allow them to build a little white house, with gilded window frames, and to die quietly in the spot where they were born. . . .

ALPINE RESORTS

Historians tell us that the first inhabitants of the Upper Engadine were Etruscans and Latins chased from Italy by the Gauls and Carthaginians, and taking refuge in these hidden altitudes. After the fall of the Empire, the inhabitants of the Engadine fell under the dominion of the Franks and Lombards, then the Dukes of Swabia; but the blood never mingled—the type remained Italian; black hair, the quick eye, the mobile countenance, the expressive features, and the supple figure.

GENEVA*

BY FRANCIS H. GRIBBLE

Straddling the Rhone, where it issues from the bluest lake in the world, looking out upon green meadows and wooded hills, backed by the dark ridge of the Salève, with the "great white mountain" visible in the distance, Geneva has the advantage of an incomparable site; and it is, from a town surveyor's point of view, well built. It has wide thoroughfares, quays, and bridges; gorgeous public monuments and well-kept public gardens; handsome theaters and museums; long rows of palatial hotels; flourishing suburbs; two railway-stations, and a casino. But all this is merely the façade—all of it quite modern; hardly any of it more than half a century old. The real historical Geneva—the little of it that remains—is hidden away in the background, where not every tourist troubles to look for it.

*From "Geneva."

SEEING EUROPE WITH FAMOUS AUTHORS

It is disappearing fast. Italian stonemasons are constantly engaged in driving lines through it. They have rebuilt, for instance, the old Corraterie, which is now the Regent Street of Geneva, famous for its confectioners' and booksellers' shops; they have destroyed, and are still destroying, other ancient slums, setting up white buildings of uniform ugliness in place of the picturesque but insanitary dwellings of the past. It is, no doubt, a very necessary reform, tho one may think that it is being executed in too utilitarian a spirit. The old Geneva was malodorous, and its death-rate was high. They had more than one Great Plague there, and their Great Fires have always left some of the worst of their slums untouched. These could not be allowed to stand in an age which studies the science and practises the art of hygiene. Yet the traveler who wants to know what the old Geneva was really like must spend a morning or two rambling among them before they are pulled down.

The old Geneva, like Jerusalem, was set upon a hill, and it is toward the top of the hill that the few buildings of historical interest are to be found. There is the cathedral—a striking object from a distance, tho the interior is hideously bare. There is the Town Hall, in which, for the convenience of notables carried in litters, the upper stories were reached by an inclined plane instead of a staircase. There is Calvin's old Academy, bearing more than a slight resemblance to certain of the smaller colleges at Oxford and Cambridge. There, too, are to be seen a few mural tablets, indicating the residences of past celebrities. In such a house Rousseau was born; in such another house

ALPINE RESORTS

—or in an older house, now demolished, on the same site—Calvin died. And toward these central points the steep and narrow, mean streets—in many cases streets of stairs—converge.

As one plunges into these streets one seems to pass back from the twentieth century to the fifteenth, and need not exercise one's imagination very severely in order to picture the town as it appeared in the old days before the Reformation. The present writer may claim permission to borrow his own description from the pages of "Lake Geneva and its Literary Landmarks:"

"Narrow streets predominated, tho there were also a certain number of open spaces—notably at the markets, and in front of the Cathedral, where there was a traffic in those relics and rosaries which Geneva was presently to repudiate with virtuous indignation. One can form an idea of the appearance of the narrow streets by imagining the oldest houses that one has seen in Switzerland all closely packed together—houses at the most three stories high, with gabled roofs, ground-floors a step or two below the level of the roadway, and huge arched doors studded with great iron nails, and looking strong enough to resist a battering-ram. Above the doors, in the case of the better houses, were the painted escutcheons of the residents, and crests were also often blazoned on the window-panes. The shops, too, and more especially the inns, flaunted gaudy signboards with ingenious devices. The Good Vinegar, the Hot Knife, the Crowned Ox, were the names of some of these; their tariff is said to have been fivepence a day for man and beast." . . . .

In the first half of the sixteenth century occurred the two events which shaped the future of Geneva; Reformation theology was accepted; political independence was achieved. Geneva it should be explained, was the fief of the duchy of Savoy; or so, at all events, the Dukes of Savoy maintained, tho the citizens were of the contrary opinion. Their view was that they owed allegiance only to their Bishops, who were the Viceroys of the Holy Roman Emperor; and even that allegiance was limited by the terms of a Charter granted in the Holy Roman Emperor's name by Bishop Adhémar de Fabri. All went fairly well until the Bishops began to play into the hands of the Dukes; but then there was friction, which rapidly became acute. A revolutionary party—the Eidgenossen, or Confederates—was formed. There was a Declaration of Independence and a civil war.

So long as the Genevans stood alone, the Duke was too strong for them. He marched into the town in the style of a conqueror, and wreaked his vengeance on as many of his enemies as he could catch. He cut off the head of Philibert Berthelier, to whom there stands a memorial on the island in the Rhone; he caused Jean Pecolat to be hung up in an absurd posture in his banqueting-hall, in order that he might mock at his discomfort while he dined; he executed, with or without preliminary torture, several less conspicuous patriots. Happily, however, some of the patriots—notably Besançon Hugues—got safely away, and succeeded in concluding threaties of alliance between Geneva and the cantons of Berne and Fribourg.

The men of Fribourg marched to Geneva, and the Duke retired. The citizens passed a resolution that he should never be allowed to enter the town again, seeing that he "never came there without playing the citizens some dirty trick or other;" and, the more effectually to prevent him from coming, they pulled down their suburbs and repaired their ramparts, one member of every household being required to lend a hand for the purpose.

Presently, owing to religious dissensions, Fribourg withdrew from the alliance. Berne, however, adhered to it, and, in due course, responded to the appeal for help by setting an army of seven thousand men in motion. The route of the seven thousand lay through the canton of Vaud, then a portion of the Duke's dominions, governed from the Castle of Chillon. Meeting with no resistance save at Yverdon, they annexed the territory, placing governors of their own in its various strongholds. The Governor of Chillon fled, leaving his garrison to surrender; and in its deepest dungeon was found the famous prisoner of Chillon, François de Bonivard. From that time forward Geneva was a free republic, owing allegiance to no higher power.

THE CASTLE OF CHILLON*

BY HARRIET BEECHER STOWE

Here I am, sitting at my window, overlooking Lake Leman. Castle Chillon, with its old conical towers, is silently pictured in the still waters. It has been a day of a thousand. We took a boat,

From "Sunny Memories of Foreign Lands."

with two oarsmen, and passed leisurely along the shores, under the cool, drooping branches of trees, to the castle, which is scarce a stone's throw from the hotel. We rowed along, close under the walls, to the ancient moat and drawbridge. There I picked a bunch of blue bells, "les clochettes," which were hanging their aerial pendants from every crevice—some blue, some white. . . .

We rowed along, almost touching the castle rock, where the wall ascends perpendicularly, and the water is said to be a thousand feet deep. We passed the loopholes that illuminate the dungeon vaults, and an old arch, now walled up, where prisoners, after having been strangled, were thrown into the lake.

Last evening we walked through the castle. An interesting Swiss woman, who has taught herself English for the benefit of her visitors, was our "cicerone." She seemed to have all the old Swiss vivacity of attachment for "liberté et patrie." She took us first into the dungeon, with the seven pillars, described by Byron. There was the pillar to which, for protecting the liberty of Geneva, Bonivard was chained. There the Duke of Savoy kept him for six years, confined by a chain four feet long. He could take only three steps, and the stone floor is deeply worn by the prints of those weary steps. Six years is so easily said; but to live them, alone, helpless, a man burning with all the fires of manhood, chained to that pillar of stone, and those three unvarying steps! Two thousand one hundred and ninety days rose and set the sun, while seed time and harvest, winter and summer, and the whole living world went on over his grave. For him no sun, no moon, no stars, no business, no

ALPINE RESORTS

friendship, no plans—nothing! The great millstone of life emptily grinding itself away!

What a power of vitality was there in Bonivard, that he did not sink in lethargy, and forget himself to stone! But he did not; it is said that when the victorious Swiss army broke in to liberate him, they cried,

"Bonivard, you are free!"

"And Geneva?"

"Geneva is free also!"

You ought to have heard the enthusiasm with which our guide told this story!

Near by are the relics of the cell of a companion of Bonivard, who made an ineffectual attempt to liberate him. On the wall are still seen sketches of saints and inscriptions by his hand. This man one day overcame his jailer, locked him in his cell, ran into the hall above, and threw himself from a window into the lake, struck a rock, and was killed instantly. One of the pillars in this vault is covered with names. I think it is Bonivard's pillar. There are the names of Byron, Hunt, Schiller, and many other celebrities.

After we left the dungeons we went up into the judgment hall, where prisoners were tried, and then into the torture chamber. Here are the pulleys by which limbs are broken; the beam, all scorched with the irons by which feet were burned; the oven where the irons were heated; and there was the stone where they were sometimes laid to be strangled, after the torture. On that stone, our guide told us, two thousand Jews, men, women, and children, had been put to death. There was also, high up, a strong beam across, where criminals were hung; and a door, now walled up, by which they were thrown into the lake. I shivered. "'Twas cruel," she said; "'twas almost as cruel as your slavery in America."*

Then she took us into a tower where was the "oubliette." Here the unfortunate prisoner was made to kneel before an image of the Virgin, while the treacherous floor, falling beneath him, precipitated him into a well forty feet deep, where he was left to die of broken limbs and starvation. Below this well was still another pit, filled with knives, into which, when they were disposed to a merciful hastening of the torture, they let him fall. The woman has been herself to the bottom of the first dungeon, and found there bones of victims. The second pit is now walled up. . . .

To-night, after sunset, we rowed to Byron's "little isle," the only one in the lake. O, the unutterable beauty of these mountains—great, purple waves, as if they had been dashed up by a mighty tempest, crested with snow-like foam! this purple sky, and crescent moon, and the lake gleaming and shimmering, and twinkling stars, while far off up the sides of a snow-topped mountain a light shines like a star—some mountaineer's candle, I suppose.

In the dark stillness we rode again over to Chillon, and paused under its walls. The frogs were croaking in the moat, and we lay rocking on the wave, and watching the dusky outlines of the towers and turrets. Then the spirit of the scene seemed to wrap me round like a cloak. Back to Geneva again. This lovely place will ever leave its image on my heart. Mountains embrace it.

*Mrs. Stowe's "Uncle Tom's Cabin" had been published about a year when this remark was made to her.

ALPINE RESORTS

BY RAIL UP THE GORNER-GRAT*

BY ARCHIBALD CAMPBELL KNOWLES

To see the splendid array of snow peaks and glaciers which makes the sky line above Zermatt, one must leave the valley and walk or climb to a higher level. An ideal spot for this is the Hôtel Riffel Alp. Both the situation and the Hôtel outrival and surpass any similar places in the Alps. "Far from the madding crowd," on a little plateau bounded by pines and pastures stands the Hôtel, some two thousand feet above Zermatt and at an altitude of over 7,000 feet. The outlook is superb, the air splendid, the quiet most restful. Two little churches, the one for Roman Catholics, the other for members of the Church of England minister to the spiritual needs of the visitors and stamp religion upon a situation grand and sublime.

Those who come here are lovers of the mountains who enjoy the open life. It is a place not so much for "les grands excursions" as for long walks, easy climbs and the beginnings of mountaineering. Many persons spend the entire day out, preferring to eat their déjeuner "informally," perched above some safe precipice, or on a glacier-bordered rock or in the shade of the cool woods, but there are always some who linger both morning and afternoon on the terrace with its far expanse of view, with the bright sunshine streaming down upon them.

One great charm of the Riffel Alp is the proximity to the snow. An hour will bring one either to the

*From "Adventures in the Alps." Published by George W. Jacobs & Co.

SEEING EUROPE WITH FAMOUS AUTHORS

Gorner Glacier or to the Findelen Glacier, while a somewhat longer time will lead to other stretches of snow and ice, where the climber may sit and survey the séracs and crevasses or walk about on the great frozen rivers. This is said to be beneficial to the nervous system as many physicians maintain that the glaciers contain a large amount of radium.

Before essaying any of the longer or harder trips however, the traveler first of all generally goes to the Gorner-Grat, the rocky ridge that runs up from Zermatt to a point 10,290 feet high. Many people still walk up, but since the railroad was built, even those who feel it to be a matter of conscience to inveigh against any kind of progress which ministers to the pleasures of the masses, are found among those who prefer to ascend by electricity. The trip up is often made very amusing as among the crowds are always some, who knowing really nothing of the place, feel it incumbent upon themselves to point out all of the peaks, in a way quite discomposing to anybody familiar with the locality or versed in geography! Quite a luxurious little hôtel now surmounts the top of the Gorner-Grat. In it, about it and above it, on the walled terrace assembles a motley crowd every clear day in summer, clad in every variety of costume, conventional and unconventional. . . .

An ordinary scene would be ruined by such a crowd, but not so the Gorner-Grat. The very majesty and magnificence of the view make one forget the vaporings of mere man, and the Glory of God, so overpoweringly revealed in those regions of perpetual snow, drives other impressions away. And if one wishes to be alone, it is easily

ALPINE RESORTS

possible by walking a little further along the ridge where some rock will shut out all sight of man and the wind will drive away the sound of voices.

It is doubtful if there is any view comparable with that of the Gorner-Grat. There is what is called a "near view," and there is also what is known as a "distant view," for completely surrounded by snow peak and glacier, the eye passes from valley to summit, resting on that wonderful stretch of shining white which forms the skyline. To say that one can count dozens of glaciers, that he can see fifty summits, that Monte Rosa, the Lyskamm, the Twins, the Breithorn, the Matterhorn, the Dent Blanche, the Weisshorn, with many other mountains of the Valais and Oberland form a complete circle of snow peaks, may establish the geography of the place but it does not convey any but the faintest picture of the sublime grandeur of the scene. . . .

An exciting experience for novices is to go with a guide from the Gorner-Grat to the Hohtäligrat and thence down to the Findelen Glacier. It looks dangerous but it is not really so, if the climber is careful, for altho there is a sheer descent on either side of the arête or ridge which leads from the one point to the other, the way is never narrow and only over easy rocks and snow.

The Hohtäligrat is almost 11,000 feet in altitude and has a splendid survey of the sky line One looks up at snow, one looks down at snow, one looks around at snow! From the beautiful summits of Monte Rosa, the eye passes in a complete circle, up and down, seeing in succession the white snow peaks, with their great glistening glaciers below, showing in strong contrast the occasional rock pyramids like the Matterhorn and the group around the Rothhorn.

THROUGH THE ST. GOTHARD INTO ITALY*

BY VICTOR TISSOT

This is Geschenen, at the entrance of the great tunnel, the meeting place of the upper gorges of the Reuss, the valley of Urseren, of the Oberalp, and of the Furka. Geschenen has now the calm tranquility of old age. But during the nine years that it took to bore the great tunnel, what juvenile activity there was here, what feverish eagerness in this village, crowded, inundated, overflowed by workmen from Italy, from Tessin, from Germany and France! One would have thought that out of that dark hole, dug out in the mountain, they were bringing nuggets of gold.

On all the roads nothing was to be seen but bands of workmen arriving, with miners' lamps hung to their old soldier's knapsacks. Nobody could tell how they were all to be lodged. One double bed was occupied in succession by twenty-four men in twenty-four hours. Some of the workmen set up their establishments in barns; in all directions movable canteens sprung up, built all awry and hardly holding together, and in mean sheds, doubtful, bad-looking places, the dis-

*From "Unknown Switzerland." Published by James Pott & Co.

honest merchant hastened to sell his adulterated brandy. . . .

The St. Gothard tunnel is about one and two-third miles longer than that of Mount Cenis, and more than three miles longer than that of Arlberg. While the train is passing with a dull rumbling sound under these gloomy vaults, let us explain how the great work of boring the Alps was accomplished.

The mechanical work of perforation was begun simultaneously on the north and south sides of the mountain, working toward the same point, so as to meet toward the middle of the boring. The waters of the Reuss and the Tessin supplied the necessary motive power for working the screws attached to machinery for compressing the air. The borers applied to the rock the piston of a cylinder made to rotate with great rapidity by the pressure of air reduced to one-twentieth of its ordinary volume; then when they had made holes sufficiently deep, they withdrew the machines and charged the mines with dynamite. Immediately after the explosion, streams of wholesome air were liberated which dissipated the smoke; then the débris was cleared away, and the borers returned to their place. The same work was thus carried on day and night, for nine years.

On the Geschenen side all went well; but on the other side, on the Italian slope, unforseen obstacles and difficulties had to be overcome. Instead of having to encounter the solid rock, they found themselves among a moving soil formed by the deposit of glaciers and broken by streams of water. Springs burst out, like the jet of a fountain, under the stroke of the pick, flooding and driving away the workmen. For twelve months they seemed to be in the midst of a lake. But nothing could damp the ardor of the contractor, Favre.

His troubles were greater still when the undertaking had almost been suspended for want of money, when the workmen struck in 1875, and, when, two years later, the village of Arola was destroyed by fire. And how many times, again and again, the mason-work of the vaulted roof gave way and fell! Certain "bad places," as they were called, cost more than nine hundred pounds per yard.

In the interior of the mountain the thermometer marked 86 degrees (Fahr.), but so long as the tunnel was still not completely bored, the workmen were sustained by a kind of fever, and made redoubled efforts. Discouragement and desertion did not appear among them till the goal was almost reached.

The great tunnel passed, we find ourselves fairly in Italy. The mulberry trees, with silky white bark and delicate, transparent leaves; the chestnuts, with enormous trunks like cathedral columns; the vine, hanging to high trellises supported by granite pillars, its festoons as capricious as the feats of those who partake too freely of its fruits; the white tufty heads of the maize tossing in the breeze; all that strong and luxuriant vegetation through which waves of moist air are passing; those flowers of rare beauty, of a grace and brilliancy that belong only to privileged zones;—all this indicates a more robust and fertile soil, and a more fervid sky than those of the upper villages which we have just left.

X

ALPINE MOUNTAIN CLIMBING

FIRST ATTEMPTS HALF A CENTURY AGO*

BY EDWARD WHYMPER

On the 23d of July, 1860, I started for my first tour of the Alps. At Zermatt I wandered in many directions, but the weather was bad and my work was much retarded. One day, after spending a long time in attempts to sketch near the Hörnli, and in futile endeavors to seize the forms of the peaks as they for a few seconds peered out from above the dense banks of woolly clouds, I determined not to return to Zermatt by the usual path, but to cross the Görner glacier to the Riffel hotel. After a rapid scramble over the polished rocks and snow-beds which skirt the base of the Theodule glacier, and wading through some of the streams which flow from it, at that time much swollen by the late rains, the first difficulty was arrived at, in the shape of a precipice about three hundred feet high. It seemed that there would be no difficulty in crossing the glacier if the cliff could be descended, but higher up and

*From "Scrambles Amongst the Alps." Mr. Whymper's later achievements in the Alps are now integral parts of the written history of notable mountain climbing feats the world over.

lower down the ice appeared, to my inexperienced eyes, to be impassable for a single person.

The general contour of the cliff was nearly perpendicular, but it was a good deal broken up, and there was little difficulty in descending by zigzagging from one mass to another. At length there was a long slab, nearly smooth, fixt at an angle of about forty degrees between two wall-sided pieces of rock; nothing, except the glacier, could be seen below. It was a very awkward place, but being doubtful if return were possible, as I had been dropping from one ledge to another, I passed at length by lying across the slab, putting the shoulder stiffly against one side and the feet against the other, and gradually wriggling down, by first moving the legs and then the back. When the bottom of the slab was gained a friendly crack was seen, into which the point of the bâton could be stuck, and I dropt down to the next piece.

It took a long time coming down that little bit of cliff, and for a few seconds it was satisfactory to see the ice close at hand. In another moment a second difficulty presented itself. The glacier swept round an angle of the cliff, and as the ice was not of the nature of treacle or thin putty, it kept away from the little bay on the edge of which I stood. We were not widely separated, but the edge of the ice was higher than the opposite edge of rock; and worse, the rock was covered with loose earth and stones which had fallen from above. All along the side of the cliff, as far as could be seen in both directions, the ice did not touch it, but there was this marginal crevasse seven feet wide and of unknown depth.

ALPINE MOUNTAIN CLIMBING

All this was seen at a glance, and almost at once I concluded that I could not jump the crevasse, and began to try along the cliff lower down, but without success, for the ice rose higher and higher, until at last farther progress was stopt by the cliffs becoming perfectly smooth. With an ax it would have been possible to cut up the side of the ice—without one, I saw there was no alternative but to return and face the jump.

It was getting toward evening, and the solemn stillness of the High Alps was broken only by the sound of rushing water or of falling rocks. If the jump should be successful, well; if not, I fell into the horrible chasm, to be frozen in, or drowned in that gurgling, rushing water. Everything depended on that jump. Again I asked myself, "Can it be done?" It must be. So, finding my stick was useless, I threw it and the sketch-book to the ice, and first retreating as far as possible, ran forward with all my might, took the leap, barely reached the other side, and fell awkwardly on my knees. At the same moment a shower of stones fell on the spot from which I had jumped.

The glacier was crossed without further trouble, but the Riffel, which was then a very small building, was crammed with tourists, and could not take me in. As the way down was unknown to me, some of the people obligingly suggested getting a man at the chalets, otherwise the path would be certainly lost in the forest. On arriving at the chalets no man could be found, and the lights of Zermatt, shining through the trees, seemed to say, "Never mind a guide, but come along down; we'll show you the way"; so off I went through the forest, going straight toward them.

The path was lost in a moment, and was never recovered. I was tript up by pine roots, I tumbled over rhododendron bushes, I fell over rocks. The night was pitch-dark, and after a time the lights of Zermatt became obscure or went out altogether. By a series of slides or falls, or evolutions more or less disagreeable, the descent through the forest was at length accomplished, but torrents of a formidable character had still to be passed before one could arrive at Zermatt. I felt my way about for hours, almost hopelessly, by an exhaustive process at last discovering a bridge, and about midnight, covered with dirt and scratches, reentered the inn which I had quitted in the morning. . . .

I descended the valley, diverging from the path at Randa to mount the slopes of the Dom (the highest of the Mischabelhörner), in order to see the Weisshorn face to face. The latter mountain is the noblest in Switzerland, and from this direction it looks especially magnificent. On its north there is a large snowy plateau that feeds the glacier of which a portion is seen from Randa, and which on more than one occasion has destroyed that village. From the direction of the Dom— that is, immediately opposite—this Bies glacier seems to descend nearly vertically; it does not do so, altho it is very steep. Its size is much less than formerly and the lower portion, now divided into three tails, clings in a strange, weird-like manner to the cliffs, to which it seems scarcely possible that it can remain attached.

Unwillingly I parted from the sight of this glorious mountain, and went down to Visp. Arriving once more in the Rhone valley, I proceeded to Viesch, and from thence ascended the Æggisch-

ALPINE MOUNTAIN CLIMBING

horn, on which unpleasant eminence I lost my way in a fog, and my temper shortly afterward. Then, after crossing the Grimsel in a severe thunderstorm, I passed on to Brienz, Interlachen and Berne, and thence to Fribourg and Morat, Neuchâtel, Martigny and the St. Bernard. The massive walls of the convent were a welcome sight as I waded through the snow-beds near the summit of the pass, and pleasant also was the courteous salutation of the brother who bade me enter.

Instead of descending to Aosta, I turned into the Val Pelline, in order to obtain views of the Dent d'Erin. The night had come on before Biona was gained, and I had to knock long and loud upon the door of the curé's house before it was opened. An old woman with querulous voice and with a large goître answered the summons, and demanded rather sharply what was wanted, but became pacific, almost good-natured, when a five-franc piece was held in her face and she heard that lodging and supper were required in exchange.

My directions asserted that a passage existed from Prerayen, at the head of this valley, to Breuil, in the Val Tournanche, and the old woman, now convinced of my respectability, busied herself to find a guide. Presently she introduced a native picturesquely attired in high-peaked hat, braided jacket, scarlet waistcoat and indigo pantaloons, who agreed to take me to the village of Val Tournanche. We set off early on the next morning, and got to the summit of the pass without difficulty. It gave me my first experience of considerable slopes of hard, steep snow, and, like all beginners, I endeavored to prop myself up with my stick, and kept it outside, instead of holding it between myself and the slope, and leaning upon it, as should have been done.

The man enlightened me, but he had, properly, a very small opinion of his employer, and it is probably on that account that, a few minutes after we had passed the summit, he said he would not go any farther and would return to Biona. All argument was useless; he stood still, and to everything that was said answered nothing but that he would go back. Being rather nervous about descending some long snow-slopes which still intervened between us and the head of the valley, I offered more pay, and he went on a little way. Presently there were some cliffs, down which we had to scramble. He called to me to stop, then shouted that he would go back, and beckoned to me to come up.

On the contrary, I waited for him to come down, but instead of doing so, in a second or two he turned round, clambered deliberately up the cliff and vanished. I supposed it was only a ruse to extort offers of more money, and waited for half an hour, but he did not appear again. This was rather embarrassing, for he carried off my knapsack. The choice of action lay between chasing him and going on to Breuil, risking the loss of my knapsack. I chose the latter course, and got to Breuil the same evening. The landlord of the inn, suspicious of a person entirely innocent of luggage, was doubtful if he could admit me, and eventually thrust me into a kind of loft, which was already occupied by guides and by hay. In later years we became good friends, and he did not hesitate to give credit and even to advance considerable sums.

ALPINE MOUNTAIN CLIMBING

My sketches from Breuil were made under difficulties; my materials had been carried off, nothing better than fine sugar-paper could be obtained, and the pencils seemed to contain more silica than plumbago. However, they were made, and the pass was again crossed, this time alone. By the following evening the old woman of Biona again produced the faithless guide. The knapsack was recovered after the lapse of several hours, and then I poured forth all the terms of abuse and reproach of which I was master. The man smiled when I called him a liar, and shrugged his shoulders when referred to as a thief, but drew his knife when spoken of as a pig.

The following night was spent at Cormayeur, and the day after I crossed the Col Ferrex to Orsières, and on the next the Tête Noir to Chamounix. The Emperor Napoleon arrived the same day, and access to the Mer de Glace was refused to tourists; but, by scrambling along the Plan des Aiguilles, I managed to outwit the guards, and to arrive at the Montanvert as the imperial party was leaving, failing to get to the Jardin the same afternoon, but very nearly succeeding in breaking a leg by dislodging great rocks on the moraine of the glacier.

From Chamounix I went to Geneva, and thence by the Mont Cenis to Turin and to the Vaudois valleys. A long and weary day had ended when Paesana was reached. The next morning I passed the little lakes which are the sources of the Po, on my way into France. The weather was stormy, and misinterpreting the dialect of some natives—who in reality pointed out the right way—I missed the track, and found myself under the cliffs of Monte Viso. A gap that was occasionally seen in the ridge connecting it with the mountains to the east tempted me up, and after a battle with a snow-slope of excessive steepness, I reached the summit. The scene was extraordinary, and, in my experience, unique. To the north there was not a particle of mist, and the violent wind coming from that direction blew one back staggering. But on the side of Italy the valleys were completely filled with dense masses of cloud to a certain level; and here—where they felt the influence of the wind—they were cut off as level as the top of a table, the ridges appearing above them.

I raced down to Abries, and went on through the gorge of the Guil to Mont Dauphin. The next day found me at La Bessée, at the junction of the Val Louise with the valley of the Durance, in full view of Mont Pelvoux. The same night I slept at Briançon, intending to take the courier on the following day to Grenoble, but all places had been secured several days beforehand, so I set out at two P.M. on the next day for a seventy-mile walk. The weather was again bad, and on the summit of the Col de Lautaret I was forced to seek shelter in the wretched little hospice. It was filled with workmen who were employed on the road, and with noxious vapors which proceeded from them. The inclemency of the weather was preferable to the inhospitality of the interior.

Outside, it was disagreeable, but grand—inside, it was disagreeable and mean. The walk was continued under a deluge of rain, and I felt the way down, so intense was the darkness, to the village of La Grave, where the people of the inn detained me forcibly. It was perhaps fortunate that they did so, for during that night blocks of rock fell at several places from the cliffs on to the road with such force that they made large holes in the macadam, which looked as if there had been explosions of gunpowder. I resumed the walk at half-past five next morning, and proceeded, under steady rain, through Bourg d'Oysans to Grenoble, arriving at the latter place soon after seven P.M., having accomplished the entire distance from Briançon in about eighteen hours of actual walking.

This was the end of the Alpine portion of my tour of 1860, on which I was introduced to the great peaks, and acquired the passion for mountain-scrambling.

FIRST TO THE TOP OF THE MATTERHORN*

BY EDWARD WHYMPER

We started from Zermatt on the 13th of July at half-past five, on a brilliant and perfectly cloudless morning. We were eight in number— Croz, old Peter and his two sons, Lord Francis Douglas, Hadow, Hudson and I. To ensure steady motion, one tourist and one native walked together. The youngest Taugwalder fell to my share, and the lad marched well, proud to be on the expedition and happy to show his powers. The

*From "Scrambles Amongst the Alps." Mr. Whymper's ascent of the Matterhorn was made in 1865. It was the first ascent ever made so far as known. Whymper died at Chamouni in 1911.

wine-bags also fell to my lot to carry, and throughout the day, after each drink, I replenished them secretly with water, so that at the next halt they were found fuller than before! This was considered a good omen, and little short of miraculous.

On the first day we did not intend to ascend to any great height, and we mounted, accordingly, very leisurely, picked up the things which were left in the chapel at the Schwarzsee at 8:20, and proceeded thence along the ridge connecting the Hörnli with the Matterhorn. At half-past eleven we arrived at the base of the actual peak, then quitted the ridge and clambered round some ledges on to the eastern face. We were now fairly upon the mountain, and were astonished to find that places which from the Riffel, or even from the Furggengletscher, looked entirely impracticable, were so easy that we could run about.

Before twelve o'clock we had found a good position for the tent, at a height of eleven thousand feet. Croz and young Peter went on to see what was above, in order to save time on the following morning. They cut across the heads of the snow-slopes which descended toward the Furggengletscher, and disappeared round a corner, but shortly afterward we saw them high up on the face, moving quickly. We others made a solid platform for the tent in a well-protected spot, and then watched eagerly for the return of the men. The stones which they upset told that they were very high, and we supposed that the way must be easy. At length, just before 3 P.M., we saw them coming down, evidently much excited. "What are they saying, Peter?" "Gentlemen, they say it is no good." But when they came near we heard a

ALPINE MOUNTAIN CLIMBING

different story: "Nothing but what was good—not a difficulty, not a single difficulty! We could have gone to the summit and returned to-day easily!"

We passed the remaining hours of daylight—some basking in the sunshine, some sketching or collecting—and when the sun went down, giving, as it departed, a glorious promise for the morrow, we returned to the tent to arrange for the night. Hudson made tea, I coffee, and we then retired each one to his blanket-bag, the Taugwalders, Lord Francis Douglas and myself occupying the tent, the others remaining, by preference, outside. Long after dusk the cliffs above echoed with our laughter and with the songs of the guides, for we were happy that night in camp, and feared no evil.

We assembled together outside the tent before dawn on the morning of the 14th, and started directly it was light enough to move. Young Peter came on with us as a guide, and his brother returned to Zermatt. We followed the route which had been taken on the previous day, and in a few minutes turned the rib which had intercepted the view of the eastern face from our tent platform. The whole of this great slope was now revealed, rising for three thousand feet like a huge natural staircase. Some parts were more and others were less easy, but we were not once brought to a halt by any serious impediment, for when an obstruction was met in front it could always be turned to the right or to the left.

For the greater part of the way there was indeed no occasion for the rope, and sometimes Hudson led, sometimes myself. At 6:20 we had attained a height of twelve thousand eight hundred feet, and halted for half an hour; we then continued the ascent without a break until 9:55, when we stopt for fifty minutes at a height of fourteen thousand feet. Twice we struck the northeastern ridge, and followed it for some little distance—to no advantage, for it was usually more rotten and steep, and always more difficult, than the face. Still, we kept near to it, lest stones perchance might fall.

We had now arrived at the foot of that part which, from the Riffelberg or from Zermatt, seems perpendicular or overhanging, and could no longer continue upon the eastern side. For a little distance we ascended by snow upon the arête—that is, the ridge—descending toward Zermatt, and then by common consent turned over to the right, or to the northern side. Before doing so we made a change in the order of ascent. Croz went first, I followed, Hudson came third; Hadow and old Peter were last. "Now," said Croz as he led off—"now for something altogether different." The work became difficult, and required caution. In some places there was little to hold, and it was desirable that those should be in front who were least likely to slip. The general slope of the mountain at this part was less than forty degrees, and snow had accumulated in, and had filled up, the interstices of the rock-face, leaving only occasional fragments projecting here and there. These were at times covered with a thin film of ice, produced from the melting and refreezing of the snow.

It was the counterpart, on a small scale, of the upper seven hundred feet of the Pointe des Écrins;

ALPINE MOUNTAIN CLIMBING

only there was this material difference—the face of the Écrins was about, or exceeded, an angle of fifty degrees, and the Matterhorn face was less than forty degrees. It was a place over which any fair mountaineers might pass in safety, and Mr. Hudson ascended this part, and, as far as I know, the entire mountain, without having the slightest assistance rendered to him upon any occasion. Sometimes, after I had taken a hand from Croz or received a pull, I turned to offer the same to Hudson, but he invariably declined, saying it was not necessary. Mr. Hadow, however, was not accustomed to this kind of work, and required continual assistance. It is only fair to say that the difficulty which he found at this part arose simply and entirely from want of experience.

This solitary difficult part was of no great extent. We bore away over it at first nearly horizontally, for a distance of about four hundred feet, then ascended directly toward the summit for about sixty feet, and then doubled back to the ridge which descends toward Zermatt. A long stride round a rather awkward corner brought us to snow once more. The last doubt vanished! The Matterhorn was ours! Nothing but two hundred feet of easy snow remained to be surmounted! . . .

The summit of the Matterhorn was formed of a rudely level ridge, about three hundred and fifty feet long. The day was one of those superlatively calm and clear ones which usually precede bad weather. The atmosphere was perfectly still and free from clouds or vapors. Mountains fifty— nay, a hundred—miles off looked sharp and near. All their details—ridge and crag, snow and glacier—stood out with faultless definition. Pleasant thoughts of happy days in bygone years came up unbidden as we recognized the old, familiar forms. All were revealed—not one of the principal peaks of the Alps was hidden. I see them clearly now —the great inner circles of giants, backed by the ranges, chains and "massifs." First came the Dent Blanche, hoary and grand; the Gabelhorn and pointed Rothborn, and then the peerless Weisshorn; the towering Mischabelhörner flanked by the Allaleinhorn, Strahlhorn and Rimpfischhorn; then Monte Rosa—with its many Spitzen—the Lyskamm and the Breithorn. Behind were the Bernese Oberland, governed by the Finsteraarhorn, the Simplon and St. Gothard groups, the Disgrazia and the Orteler. Toward the south we looked down to Chivasso on the plain of Piedmont, and far beyond. The Viso—one hundred miles away—seemed close upon us; the Maritime Alps —one hundred and thirty miles distant—were free from haze.

Then came into view my first love—the Pelvoux; the Écrins and the Meije; the clusters of the Graians; and lastly, in the west, gorgeous in the full sunlight, rose the monarch of all—Mont Blanc. Ten thousand feet beneath us were the green fields of Zermatt, dotted with chalets, from which blue smoke rose lazily. Eight thousand feet below, on the other side, were the pastures of Breuil. There were forests black and gloomy, and meadows bright and lively; bounding waterfalls and tranquil lakes; fertile lands and savage wastes; sunny plains and frigid plateaux. There were the most rugged forms and the most graceful outlines —bold, perpendicular cliffs and gentle, undulating slopes; rocky mountains and snowy mountains, somber and solemn or glittering and white, with walls, turrets, pinnacles, pyramids, domes, cones and spires! There was every combination that the world can give, and every contrast that the heart could desire. We remained on the summit for one hour—

One crowded hour of glorious life.

THE LORD FRANCIS DOUGLAS TRAGEDY*

BY EDWARD WHYMPER

We began to prepare for the descent. Hudson and I again consulted as to the best and safest arrangement of the party. We agreed that it would be best for Croz to go first, and Hadow second; Hudson, who was almost equal to a guide in sureness of foot, wished to be third; Lord Francis Douglas was placed next, and old Peter, the strongest of the remainder, after him. I suggested to Hudson that we should attach a rope to the rocks on our arrival at the difficult bit, and hold it as we descended, as an additional protection. He approved the idea, but it was not definitely settled that it should be done. The party was being arranged in the above order while I was sketching the summit, and they had finished, and were waiting for me to be tied in line, when some one

*From "Scrambles Amongst the Alps." The loss of Douglas and three other men, as here described, occurred during the descent of the Matterhorn following the ascent described by Mr. Whymper in the preceding article.

remembered that our names had not been left in a bottle. They requested me to write them down, and moved off while it was being done.

A few minutes afterward I tied myself to young Peter, ran down after the others, and caught them just as they were commencing the descent of the difficult part. Great care was being taken. Only one man was moving at a time; when he was firmly planted, the next advanced, and so on. They had not, however, attached the additional rope to rocks, and nothing was said about it. The suggestion was not made for my own sake, and I am not sure that it even occurred to me again. For some little distance we followed the others, detached from them, and should have continued so had not Lord Francis Douglas asked me, about 3 P.M., to tie on to old Peter, as he feared, he said, that Taugwalder would not be able to hold his ground if a slip occurred.

A few minutes later a sharp-eyed lad ran into the Monte Rosa hotel to Seiler,[*] saying that he had seen an avalanche fall from the summit of the Matterhorn on to the Matterhorngletscher. The boy was reproved for telling such idle stories; he was right, nevertheless, and this was what he saw.

Michael Croz had laid aside his ax, and in order to give Mr. Hadow greater security was absolutely taking hold of his legs and putting his feet, one by one, into their proper positions. As far as I know, no one was actually descending. I can not speak with certainty, because the two leading men were partially hidden from my sight by

[*] That is, down in the village of Zermatt. Seiler was a well-known innkeeper of that time. Other Seilers still keep inns at Zermatt.

ALPINE MOUNTAIN CLIMBING

an intervening mass of rock, but it is my belief, from the movements of their shoulders, that Croz, having done as I have said, was in the act of turning round to go down a step or two himself; at the moment Mr. Hadow slipt, fell against him and knocked him over.

I heard one startled exclamation from Croz, then saw him and Mr. Hadow flying downward; in another moment Hudson was dragged from his steps, and Lord Francis Douglas immediately after him. All this was the work of a moment. Immediately we heard Croz's exclamation, old Peter and I planted ourselves as firmly as the rocks would permit; the rope was taut between us, and the jerk came on us both as one man. We held, but the rope broke midway between Taugwalder and Lord Francis Douglas. For a few seconds we saw our unfortunate companions sliding downward on their backs, and spreading out their hands, endeavoring to save themselves. They passed from our sight uninjured, disappeared one by one, and fell from precipice to precipice on to the Matterhorngletscher below, a distance of nearly four thousand feet in height. From the moment the rope broke it was impossible to help them.

So perished our comrades! For the space of half an hour we remained on the spot without moving a single step. The two men, paralyzed by terror, cried like infants, and trembled in such a manner as to threaten us with the fate of the others. Old Peter rent the air with exclamations of "Chamounix!—oh, what will Chamounix say?" He meant, Who would believe that Croz could fall? The young man did nothing but scream or sob, "We are lost! we are lost!" Fixt between the two, I could move neither up nor down. I begged young Peter to descend, but he dared not. Unless he did, we could not advance. Old Peter became alive to the danger, and swelled the cry, "We are lost! we are lost!"

The father's fear was natural—he trembled for his son; the young man's fear was cowardly—he thought of self alone. At last old Peter summoned up courage, and changed his position to a rock to which he could fix the rope; the young man then descended, and we all stood together. Immediately we did so, I asked for the rope which had given way, and found, to my surprise—indeed, to my horror—that it was the weakest of the three ropes. It was not brought, and should not have been employed, for the purpose for which it was used. It was old rope, and, compared with the others, was feeble. It was intended as a reserve, in case we had to leave much rope behind attached to rocks. I saw at once that a serious question was involved, and made them give me the end. It had broken in mid-air, and it did not appear to have sustained previous injury.

For more than two hours afterward I thought almost every moment that the next would be my last, for the Taugwalders, utterly unnerved, were not only incapable of giving assistance, but were in such a state that a slip might have been expected from them at any moment. After a time we were able to do that which should have been done at first, and fixt rope to firm rocks, in addition to being tied together. These ropes were cut from time to time, and were left behind. Even with their assurance the men were afraid to proceed, and several times old Peter

ALPINE MOUNTAIN CLIMBING

turned with ashy face and faltering limbs, and said with terrible emphasis, "I can not!"

About 6 P.M. we arrived at the snow upon the ridge descending toward Zermatt, and all peril was over. We frequently looked, but in vain, for traces of our unfortunate companions; we bent over the ridge and cried to them, but no sound returned. Convinced at last that they were within neither sight nor hearing, we ceased from our useless efforts, and, too cast down for speech, silently gathered up our things, preparatory to continuing the descent.

When lo! a mighty arch appeared, rising above the Lyskamm high into the sky. Pale, colorless and noiseless, but perfectly sharp and defined, except where it was lost in the clouds, this unearthly apparition seemed like a vision from another world, and almost appalled we watched with amazement the gradual development of two vast crosses, one on either side. If the Taugwalders had not been the first to perceive it, I should have doubted my senses. They thought it had some connection with the accident, and I, after a while, that it might bear some relations to ourselves. But our movements had no effect upon it. The spectral forms remained motionless. It was a fearful and wonderful sight, unique in my experience, and impressive beyond description, at such a moment....

Night fell, and for an hour the descent was continued in the darkness. At half-past nine a resting-place was found, and upon a wretched slab, barely large enough to hold three, we passed six miserable hours. At daybreak the descent was resumed, and from the Hornli ridge we ran down to the chalets of Buhl and on to Zermatt. Seiler met me at his door, and followed in silence to my room: "What is the matter?" "The Taugwalders and I have returned." He did not need more, and burst into tears, but lost no time in lamentations, and set to work to arouse the village.

Ere long a score of men had started to ascend the Hohlicht heights, above Kalbermatt and Z'Mutt, which commanded the plateau of the Matterhorngletscher. They returned after six hours, and reported that they had seen the bodies lying motionless on the snow. This was on Saturday, and they proposed that we should leave on Sunday evening, so as to arrive upon the plateau at daybreak on Monday. We started at 2 A.M. on Sunday, the 16th, and followed the route that we had taken on the previous Thursday as far as the Hornli. From thence we went down to the right of the ridge, and mounted through the "séracs" of the Matterhorngletscher. By 8:30 we had got to the plateau at the top of the glacier, and within sight of the corner in which we knew my companions must be. As we saw one weather-beaten man after another raise the telescope, turn deadly pale and pass it on without a word to the next, we knew that all hope was gone. We approached. They had fallen below as they had fallen above—Croz a little in advance, Hadow near him, and Hudson behind, but of Lord Francis Douglas we could see nothing. We left them where they fell, buried in snow at the base of the grandest cliff of the most majestic mountain of the Alps.

*The body of Douglas has never been recovered. It is believed to lie buried deep in some crevasse in one of the great glaciers that emerge from the base of the Matterhorn.

ALPINE MOUNTAIN CLIMBING

AN ASCENT OF MONTE ROSA*

BY JOHN TYNDALL

On Monday, the 9th of August, we reached the Riffel, and, by good fortune on the evening of the same day, my guide's brother, the well-known Ulrich Lauener, also arrived at the hotel on his return from Monte Rosa. From him we obtained all the information possible respecting the ascent, and he kindly agreed to accompany us a little way the next morning, to put us on the right track. At three A.M. the door of my bedroom opened, and Christian Lauener announced to me that the weather was sufficiently good to justify an attempt. The stars were shining overhead; but Ulrich afterward drew our attention to some heavy clouds which clung to the mountains on the other side of the valley of the Visp; remarking that the weather might continue fair throughout the day, but that these clouds were ominous. At four o'clock we were on our way, by which time a gray stratus cloud had drawn itself across the neck of the Matterhorn, and soon afterward another of the same nature encircled his waist. We proceeded past the Riffelhorn to the ridge above the Görner Glacier, from which Monte Rosa was visible from top to bottom, and where an animated conversation in Swiss dialect commenced.

Ulrich described the slopes, passes, and precipices, which were to guide us; and Christian de-

*From "The Glaciers of the Alps." Prof. Tyndall made this ascent in 1858. Monte Rosa stands quite near the Matterhorn. Each is reached from Zermatt by the Gorner-Grat.

manded explanations, until he was finally able to declare to me that his knowledge was sufficient. We then bade Ulrich good-by, and went forward. All was clear about Monte Rosa, and the yellow morning light shone brightly upon its uppermost snows. Beside the Queen of the Alps was the huge mass of the Lyskamm, with a saddle stretching from the one to the other; next to the Lyskamm came two white, rounded mounds, smooth and pure, the Twins Castor and Pollux, and further to the right again the broad, brown flank of the Breithorn. Behind us Mont Cervin* gathered the clouds more thickly round him, until finally his grand obelisk was totally hidden. We went along the mountain side for a time, and then descended to the glacier.

The surface was hard frozen, and the ice crunched loudly under our feet. There was a hollowness and volume in the sound which require explanation; and this, I think, is furnished by the remarks of Sir John Herschel on those hollow sounds at the Solfaterra, near Naples, from which travelers have inferred the existence of cavities within the mountain. At the place where these sounds are heard the earth is friable, and, when struck, the concussion is reinforced and lengthened by the partial echoes from the surfaces of the fragments. The conditions for a similar effect exist upon the glacier, for the ice is disintegrated to a certain depth, and from the innumerable places of rupture little reverberations are sent, which give a length and hollowness to the sound produced by the crushing of the fragments on the surface.

*Another name for the Matterhorn.

ALPINE MOUNTAIN CLIMBING

We looked to the sky at intervals, and once a meteor slid across it, leaving a train of sparks behind. The blue firmament, from which the stars shone down so brightly when we rose, was more and more invaded by clouds, which advanced upon us from our rear, while before us the solemn heights of Monte Rosa were bathed in rich yellow sunlight. As the day advanced the radiance crept down toward the valleys; but still those stealthy clouds advanced like a besieging army, taking deliberate possession of the summits, one after another, while gray skirmishers moved through the air above us. The play of light and shadow upon Monte Rosa was at times beautiful, bars of gloom and zones of glory shifting and alternating from top to bottom of the mountain.

At five o'clock a gray cloud alighted on the shoulder of the Lyskamm, which had hitherto been warmed by the lovely yellow light. Soon afterward we reached the foot of Monte Rosa, and passed from the glacier to a slope of rocks, whose rounded forms and furrowed surfaces showed that the ice of former ages had moved over them; the granite was now coated with lichens, and between the bosses where mold could rest were patches of tender moss. As we ascended a peal to the right announced the descent of an avalanche from the Twins; it came heralded by clouds of ice-dust, which resembled the sphered masses of condensed vapor which issue from a locomotive.

A gentle snow-slope brought us to the base of a precipice of brown rocks, round which we wound; the snow was in excellent order, and the chasms were so firmly bridged by the frozen mass that no caution was necessary in crossing them. Surmounting a weathered cliff to our left, we paused upon the summit to look upon the scene around us. The snow gliding insensibly from the mountains, or discharged in avalanches from the precipices which it overhung, filled the higher valleys with pure white glaciers, which were rifted and broken here and there, exposing chasms and precipices from which gleamed the delicate blue of the half-formed ice. Sometimes, however, the "névés" spread over wide spaces without a rupture or wrinkle to break the smoothness of the superficial snow. The sky was now, for the most part, overcast, but through the residual blue spaces the sun at intervals poured light over the rounded bosses of the mountain.

At half-past seven o'clock we reached another precipice of rock, to the left of which our route lay, and here Lauener proposed to have some refreshment; after which we went on again. The clouds spread more and more, leaving at length mere specks and patches of blue between them. Passing some high peaks, formed by the dislocation of the ice, we came to a place where the "névé" was rent by crevasses, on the walls of which the stratification, due to successive snowfalls, was thrown with great beauty and definition. Between two of these fissures our way now lay; the wall of one of them was hollowed out longitudinally midway down, thus forming a roof above and a ledge below, and from roof to ledge stretched a railing of cylindrical icicles, as if intended to bolt them together. A cloud now for the first time touched the summit of Monte Rosa, and sought to cling to it, but in a minute it dispersed in shattered fragments, as if dashed to pieces for its

ALPINE MOUNTAIN CLIMBING

presumption. The mountain remained for a time clear and triumphant, but the triumph was short-lived; like suitors that will not be repelled, the dusky vapors came; repulse after repulse took place, and the sunlight gushed down upon the heights, but it was manifest that the clouds gained ground in the conflict.

Until about a quarter-past nine o'clock our work was mere child's play, a pleasant morning stroll along the flanks of the mountain; but steeper slopes now rose above us, which called for more energy, and more care in the fixing of the feet. Looked at from below, some of these slopes appeared precipitous; but we were too well acquainted with the effect of fore-shortening to let this daunt us. At each step we dug our batons into the deep snow. When first driven in, the batons* "dipt" from us, but were brought, as we walked forward, to the vertical, and finally beyond it at the other side. The snow was thus forced aside, a rubbing of the staff against it, and of the snow-particles against each other, being the consequence. We had thus perpetual rupture and regelation; while the little sounds consequent upon rupture reinforced by the partial echoes from the surfaces of the granules, were blended together to a note resembling the lowing of cows.

Hitherto I had paused at intervals to make notes, or to take an angle; but these operations now ceased, not from want of time, but from pure dislike; for when the eye has to act the part of a sentinel who feels that at any moment the

*My staff was always the handle of an ax an inch or two longer than an ordinary walking-stick.—Author's note.

enemy may be upon him; when the body must be balanced with precision, and legs and arms, besides performing actual labor, must be kept in readiness for possible contingencies; above all, when you feel that your safety depends upon yourself alone, and that, if your footing gives way, there is no strong arm behind ready to be thrown between you and destruction; under such circumstances the relish for writing ceases, and you are willing to hand over your impressions to the safe-keeping of memory.

From the vast boss which constitutes the lower portion of Monte Rosa cliffy edges run upward to the summit. Were the snow removed from these we should, I doubt not, see them as toothed or serrated crags, justifying the term "kamm," or "comb," applied to such edges by the Germans. Our way now lay along such a "kamm," the cliffs of which had, however, caught the snow, and been completely covered by it, forming an edge like the ridge of a house-roof, which sloped steeply upward. On the Lyskamm side of the edge there was no footing, and if a human body fell over here, it would probably pass through a vertical space of some thousands of feet, falling or rolling, before coming to rest. On the other side the snow-slope was less steep, but excessively perilous-looking, and intersected by precipices of ice. Dense clouds now enveloped us, and made our position far uglier than if it had been fairly illuminated. The valley below us was one vast cauldron, filled with precipitated vapor, which came seething at times up the sides of the mountain. Sometimes this fog would clear away, and the light would gleam from the dislocated glaciers.

ALPINE MOUNTAIN CLIMBING

My guide continually admonished me to make my footing sure, and to fix at each step my staff firmly in the consolidated snow. At one place, for a short steep ascent, the slope became hard ice, and our position a very ticklish one. We hewed our steps as we moved upward, but were soon glad to deviate from the ice to a position scarcely less awkward. The wind had so acted upon the snow as to fold it over the edge of the kamm, thus causing it to form a kind of cornice, which overhung the precipice on the Lyskamm side of the mountain. This cornice now bore our weight; its snow had become somewhat firm, but it was yielding enough to permit the feet to sink in it a little way, and thus secure us at least against the danger of slipping. Here, also, at each step we drove our batons firmly into the snow, availing ourselves of whatever help they could render.

Once, while thus securing my anchorage, the handle of my hatchet went right through the cornice on which we stood, and, on withdrawing it, I could see through the aperture into the cloud-crammed gulf below. We continued ascending until we reached a rock protruding from the snow, and here we halted for a few minutes. Lauener looked upward through the fog. "According to all description," he observed, "this ought to be the last kamm of the mountain; but in this obscurity we can see nothing." Snow began to fall, and we recommenced our journey, quitting the rocks and climbing again along the edge. Another hour brought us to a crest of cliffs, at which, to our comfort, the kamm appeared to cease, and other climbing qualities were demanded of us.

On the Lyskamm side, as I have said, rescue

would be out of the question, should the climber go over the edge. On the other side of the edge rescue seemed possible, tho the slope, as stated already, was most dangerously steep. I now asked Lauener what he would have done, supposing my footing to have failed on the latter slope. He did not seem to like the question, but said that he should have considered well for a moment and then have sprung after me; but he exhorted me to drive all such thoughts away. I laughed at him, and this did more to set his mind at rest than any formal profession of courage could have done.

We were now among rocks; we climbed cliffs and descended them, and advanced sometimes with our feet on narrow ledges, holding tightly on to other ledges by our fingers; sometimes, cautiously balanced, we moved along edges of rock with precipices on both sides. Once, in getting round a crag, Lauener shook a book from his pocket; it was arrested by a rock about sixty or eighty feet below us. He wished to regain it, but I offered to supply its place, if he thought the descent too dangerous. He said he would make the trial, and parted from me. I thought it useless to remain idle. A cleft was before me, through which I must pass; so pressing my knees and back against its opposite sides, I gradually worked myself to the top. I descended the other face of the rock, and then, through a second ragged fissure, to the summit of another pinnacle. The highest point of the mountain was now at hand, separated from me merely by a short saddle, carved by weathering out the crest of the mountain. I could hear Lauener clattering after me, through the rocks behind. I dropt down upon the saddle, crossed it, climb-

ALPINE MOUNTAIN CLIMBING

ed the opposite cliff, and "die höchste Spitze" of Monte Rosa was won.

Lauener joined me immediately, and we mutually congratulated each other on the success of the ascent. The residue of the bread and meat was produced, and a bottle of tea was also appealed to. Mixed with a little cognac, Lauener declared that he had never tasted anything like it. Snow fell thickly at intervals, and the obscurity was very great; occasionally this would lighten and permit the sun to shed a ghastly dilute light upon us through the gleaming vapor. I put my boiling-water apparatus in order, and fixt it in a corner behind a ledge; the shelter was, however, insufficient, so I placed my hat above the vessel. The boiling-point was 184.92 deg. Fahr., the ledge on which the instrument stood being five feet below the highest point of the mountain.

The ascent from the Riffel Hotel occupied us about seven hours, nearly two of which were spent upon the kamm and crest. Neither of us felt in the least degree fatigued; I, indeed, felt so fresh, that had another Monte Rosa been planted on the first, I should have continued the climb without hesitation, and with strong hopes of reaching the top. I experienced no trace of mountain sickness, lassitude, shortness of breath, heart-beat, or headache; nevertheless the summit of Monte Rosa is 15,284 feet high, being less than 500 feet lower than Mont Blanc. It is, I think, perfectly certain, that the rarefaction of the air at this height is not sufficient of itself to produce the symptoms referred to; physical exertion must be superadded.

SEEING EUROPE WITH FAMOUS AUTHORS

MONT BLANC ASCENDED, HUXLEY GOING PART WAY*

BY JOHN TYNDALL

The way for a time was excessively rough,† our route being overspread with the fragments of peaks which had once reared themselves to our left, but which frost and lightning had shaken to pieces, and poured in granite avalanches down the mountain. We were sometimes among huge, angular boulders, and sometimes amid lighter shingle, which gave way at every step, thus forcing us to shift our footing incessantly. Escaping from these we crossed the succession of secondary glaciers which lie at the feet of the Aiguilles, and, having secured firewood, found ourselves, after some hours of hard work, at the Pierre l'Echelle. Here we were furnished with leggings of coarse woolen cloth to keep out the snow; they were tied under the knees and quite tightly again over the insteps, so that the legs were effectually protected. We had some refreshment, possest ourselves of the ladder, and entered upon the glacier.

The ice was excessively fissured; we crossed

*From "The Glaciers of the Alps."
†That is, after having ascended the mountain to a point some distance beyond the Mer de Glace, to which the party had ascended from Chamouni, Huxley and Tyndall were both engaged in a study of the causes of the movement of glaciers, but Tyndall gave it most attention. One of Tyndall's feats in the Alps was to make the first recorded ascent of the Weisshorn. It is said that "traces of his influence remain in Switzerland to this day."

crevasses and crept round slippery ridges, cutting steps in the ice wherever climbing was necessary. This rendered our progress very slow. Once, with the intention of lending a helping hand, I stept forward upon a block of granite which happened to be poised like a rocking stone upon the ice, tho I did not know it; it treacherously turned under me; I fell, but my hands were in instant requisition, and I escaped with a bruise, from which, however, the blood oozed angrily. We found the ladder necessary in crossing some of the chasms, the iron spikes at its end being firmly driven into the ice at one side, while the other end rested on the opposite side of the fissure. The middle portion of the glacier was not difficult. Mounds of ice rose beside us right and left, which were sometimes split into high towers and gaunt-looking pyramids, while the space between was unbroken.

Twenty minutes' walking brought us again to a fissured portion of the glacier, and here our porter left the ladder on the ice behind him. For some time I was not aware of this, but we were soon fronted by a chasm to pass which we were in consequence compelled to make a long and dangerous circuit amid crests of crumbling ice. This accomplished, we hoped that no repetition of the process would occur, but we speedily came to a second fissure, where it was necessary to step from a projecting end of ice to a mass of soft snow which overhung the opposite side. Simond could reach this snow with his long-handled ax; he beat it down to give it rigidity, but it was exceedingly tender, and as he worked at it he continued to express his fears that it would not bear us. I was the lightest of the party, and therefore tested the passage first; being partially lifted by Simond on the end of his ax, I crossed the fissure, obtained some anchorage at the other side, and helped the others over. We afterward ascended until another chasm, deeper and wider than any we had hitherto encountered, arrested us. We walked alongside of it in search of a snow-bridge, which we at length found, but the keystone of the arch had, unfortunately, given way, leaving projecting eaves of snow at both sides, between which we could look into the gulf, till the gloom of its deeper portions cut the vision short.

Both sides of the crevasse were sounded, but no sure footing was obtained; the snow was beaten and carefully trodden down as near to the edge as possible, but it finally broke away from the foot and fell into the chasm. One of our porters was short-legged and a bad iceman; the other was a daring fellow, and he now threw the knapsack from his shoulders, came to the edge of the crevasse, looked into it, but drew back again. After a pause he repeated the act, testing the snow with his feet and staff. I looked at the man as he stood beside the chasm manifestly undecided as to whether he should take the step upon which his life would hang, and thought it advisable to put a stop to such perilous play. I accordingly interposed, the man withdrew from the crevasse, and he and Simond descended to fetch the ladder.

While they were away Huxley sat down upon

ALPINE MOUNTAIN CLIMBING

the ice, with an expression of fatigue stamped upon his countenance; the spirit and the muscles were evidently at war, and the resolute will mixed itself strangely with the sense of peril and feeling of exhaustion. He had been only two days with us, and, tho his strength is great, he had had no opportunity of hardening himself by previous exercise upon the ice for the task which he had undertaken. The ladder now arrived, and we crossed the crevasse. I was intentionally the last of the party, Huxley being immediately in front of me. The determination of the man disguised his real condition from everybody but himself, but I saw that the exhausting journey over the boulders and débris had been too much for his London limbs.

Converting my waterproof haversack into a cushion, I made him sit down upon it at intervals, and by thus breaking the steep ascent into short stages we reached the cabin of the Grands Mulets together. Here I spread a rug on the boards, and, placing my bag for a pillow, he lay down, and after an hour's profound sleep he rose refreshed and well; but still he thought it wise not to attempt the ascent farther. Our porters left us; a baton was stretched across the room over the stove, and our wet socks and leggings were thrown across it to dry; our boots were placed around the fire, and we set about preparing our evening meal. A pan was placed upon the fire, and filled with snow, which in due time melted and boiled; I ground some chocolate and placed it in the pan, and afterward ladled the beverage into the vessels we possest, which consisted of two earthen dishes and the metal cases of our brandy flasks. After supper Simond went out to inspect the glacier, and was observed by Huxley, as twilight fell, in a state of deep contemplation beside a crevasse.

Gradually the stars appeared, but as yet no moon. Before lying down we went out to look at the firmament, and noticed, what I supposed has been observed to some extent by everybody, that the stars near the horizon twinkled busily, while those near the zenith shone with a steady light. One large star, in particular, excited our admiration; it flashed intensely, and changed color incessantly, sometimes blushing like a ruby, and again gleaming like an emerald. A determinate color would sometimes remain constant for a sensible time, but usually the flashes followed each other in very quick succession.

Three planks were now placed across the room near the stove, and upon these, with their rugs folded round them, Huxley and Hirst stretched themselves, while I nestled on the boards at the most distant end of the room. We rose at eleven o'clock, renewed the fire and warmed ourselves, after which we lay down again. I, at length, observed a patch of pale light upon the wooden wall of the cabin, which had entered through a hole in the end of the edifice, and rising found that it was past one o'clock. The cloudless moon was shining over the wastes of snow, and the scene outside was at once wild, grand, and beautiful.

Breakfast was soon prepared, tho not without difficulty; we had no candles, they had been forgotten; but I fortunately possest a box of wax matches, of which Huxley took charge, pa-

ALPINE MOUNTAIN CLIMBING

tiently igniting them in succession, and thus giving us a tolerably continuous light. We had some tea, which had been made at the Montanvert,* and carried to the Grands Mulets in a bottle. My memory of that tea is not pleasant; it had been left a whole night in contact with its leaves, and smacked strongly of tannin. The snow-water, moreover, with which we diluted it was not pure, but left a black residuum at the bottom of the dishes in which the beverage was served. The few provisions deemed necessary being placed in Simond's knapsack, at twenty minutes past two o'clock we scrambled down the rocks, leaving Huxley behind us.

The snow was hardened by the night's frost, and we were cheered by the hope of being able to accomplish the ascent with comparatively little labor. We were environed by an atmosphere of perfect purity; the larger stars hung like gems above us, and the moon, about half full, shone with wondrous radiance in the dark firmament. One star in particular, which lay eastward from the moon, suddenly made its appearance above one of the Aiguilles, and burned there with unspeakable splendor. We turned once toward the Mulets, and saw Huxley's form projected against the sky as he stood upon a pinnacle of rock; he gave us a last wave of the hand and descended, while we receded from him into the solitudes.

The evening previous our guide had examined the glacier for some distance, his progress having been arrested by a crevasse. Beside this we

*A hotel overlooking the Mer de Glace and a headquarters for mountaineers now as then.

153

soon halted: it was spanned at one place by a bridge of snow, which was of too light a structure to permit of Simond's testing it alone; we therefore paused while our guide uncoiled a rope and tied us all together. The moment was to me a peculiarly solemn one. Our little party seemed so lonely and so small amid the silence and the vastness of the surrounding scene. We were about to try our strength under unknown conditions, and as the various possibilities of the enterprise crowded on the imagination, a sense of responsibility for a moment opprest me. But as I looked aloft and saw the glory of the heavens, my heart lightened, and I remarked cheerily to Hirst that Nature seemed to smile upon our work. "Yes," he replied, in a calm and earnest voice, "and, God willing, we shall accomplish it."

A pale light now overspread the eastern sky, which increased, as we ascended, to a daffodil tinge; this afterward heightened to orange, deepening at one extremity into red, and fading at the other into a pure, ethereal hue to which it would be difficult to assign a special name. Higher up the sky was violet, and this changed by insensible degrees into the darkling blue of the zenith, which had to thank the light of moon and stars alone for its existence. We wound steadily for a time through valleys of ice, climbed white and slippery slopes, crossed a number of crevasses, and after some time found ourselves beside a chasm of great depth and width, which extended right and left as far as we could see. We turned to the left, and marched along its edge in search of a "pont";

ALPINE MOUNTAIN CLIMBING

but matters became gradually worse; other crevasses joined on to the first one, and the further we proceeded the more riven and dislocated the ice became.

At length we reached a place where further advance was impossible. Simond, in his difficulty complained of the want of light, and wished us to wait for the advancing day; I, on the contrary, thought that we had light enough and ought to make use of it. Here the thought occurred to me that Simond, having been only once before to the top of the mountain, might not be quite clear about the route; the glacier, however, changes within certain limits from year to year, so that a general knowledge was all that could be expected, and we trusted to our own muscles to make good any mistake in the way of guidance.

We now turned and retraced our steps along the edges of chasms where the ice was disintegrated and insecure, and succeeded at length in finding a bridge which bore us across the crevasse. This error caused us the loss of an hour, and after walking for this time we could cast a stone from the point we had attained to the place whence we had been compelled to return.

Our way now lay along the face of a steep incline of snow, which was cut by the fissure we had just passed, in a direction parallel to our route. On the heights to our right, loose icecrags seemed to totter, and we passed two tracks over which the frozen blocks had rushed some short time previously. We were glad to get out of the range of these terrible projectiles, and still more so to escape the vicinity of that ugly crevasse. To be killed in the open air would be a luxury, compared with having the life squeezed out of one in the horrible gloom of these chasms. The blush of the coming day became more and more intense; still the sun himself did not appear, being hidden from us by the peaks of the Aiguille du Midi, which were drawn clear and sharp against the brightening sky. Right under this Aiguille were heaps of snow smoothly rounded and constituting a portion of the sources whence the Glacier du Géant is fed; these, as the day advanced, bloomed with a rosy light. We reached the Petit Plateau, which we found covered with the remains of ice avalanches; above us upon the crest of the mountain rose three mighty bastions, divided from each other by deep, vertical rents, with clean smooth walls, across which the lines of annual bedding were drawn like courses of masonry. From these, which incessantly renew themselves, and from the loose and broken ice-crags near them, the boulders amid which we now threaded our way had been discharged. When they fall their descent must be sublime.

The snow had been gradually getting deeper, and the ascent more wearisome, but superadded to this at the Petit Plateau was the uncertainty of the footing between the blocks of ice. In many places the space was merely covered by a thin crust, which, when trod upon, instantly yielded and we sank with a shock sometimes to the hips. Our way next lay up a steep incline to the Grand Plateau, the depth and tenderness of the snow augmenting as we ascended. We had not yet seen the sun, but as we attained the brow which forms the entrance to the Grand Plateau, he hung his disk upon a spike of rock to our left, and, surrounded by a glory of interference spectra of the most gorgeous colors, blazed down upon us. On the Grand Plateau we halted and had our frugal refreshment.

At some distance to our left was the crevasse into which Dr. Hamel's three guides were precipitated by an avalanche in 1820; they are still entombed in the ice, and some future explorer may, perhaps, see them disgorged lower down, fresh and undecayed. They can hardly reach the surface until they pass the snow-line of the glacier, for above this line the quantity of snow that annually falls being in excess of the quantity melted, the tendency would be to make the ice-covering above them thicker. But it is also possible that the waste of the ice underneath may have brought the bodies to the bed of the glacier, where their very bones may have been ground to mud by an agency which the hardest rocks can not withstand.

As the sun poured his light upon the Plateau the little snow-facets sparkled brilliantly, sometimes with a pure white light, and at others with prismatic colors. Contrasted with the white spaces above and around us were the dark mountains on the opposite side of the valley of Chamouni, around which fantastic masses of cloud were beginning to build themselves. Mont Buet, with its cone of snow, looked small, and the Brevent altogether mean; the limestone bastions of the Fys, however, still presented a front of gloom and grandeur. We traversed the Grand Plateau, and at length reached the base of an extremely steep incline which stretched upward toward the Corridor. Here, as if produced by a fault, consequent upon the sinking of the ice in front, rose a vertical precipice, from the coping of which vast stalactites of ice depended.

Previous to reaching this place I had noticed a haggard expression upon the countenance of our guide, which was now intensified by the prospect of the ascent before him. Hitherto he had always been in front, which was certainly the most fatiguing position. I felt that I must now take the lead, so I spoke cheerily to the man and placed him behind me. Marking a number of points upon the slope as resting places, I went swiftly from one to the other, The surface of the snow had been partially melted by the sun and then refrozen, thus forming a superficial crust, which bore the weight up to a certain point, and then suddenly gave way, permitting the leg to sink to above the knee. The shock consequent on this, and the subsequent effort necessary to extricate the leg, were extremely fatiguing. My motion was complained of as too quick, and my tracks as imperfect; I moderated the former, and to render my footholes broad and sure, I stamped upon the frozen crust, and twisted my legs in the soft mass underneath,—a terribly exhausting process. I thus led the way to the base of the Rochers Rouges, up to which the fault already referred to had prolonged itself as a crevasse, which was roofed at one place by a most dangerous-looking snow-bridge.

Simond came to the front; I drew his atten-

ALPINE MOUNTAIN CLIMBING

tion to the state of the snow, and proposed climbing the Rochers Rouges; but, with a promptness unusual with him, he replied that this was impossible; the bridge was our only means of passing, and we must try it. We grasped our ropes, and dug our feet firmly into the snow to check the man's descent if the "pont" gave way, but to our astonishment it bore him, and bore us safely after him. The slope which we had now to ascend had the snow swept from its surface, and was therefore firm ice. It was most dangerously steep, and, its termination being the fretted coping of the precipice to which I have referred, if we slid downward we should shoot over this and be dashed to pieces upon the ice below.* Simond, who had come to the front to cross the crevasse, was now engaged in cutting steps, which he made deep and large, so that they might serve us on our return. But the listless strokes of his ax proclaimed his exhaustion; so I took the implement out of his hands, and changed places with him. Step after step was hewn, but the top of the Corridor appeared ever to recede from us.

Hirst was behind, unoccupied, and could thus turn his thoughts to the peril of our position; he "felt" the angle on which we hung, and saw the edge of the precipice, to which less than a quarter of a minute's slide would carry us, and

*Those acquainted with the mountain will at once recognize the grave error here committed. In fact, on starting from the Grands Mulets we had crossed the glacier too far, and throughout were much too close to the Dôme du Gouté.—Author's note.

for the first time during the journey he grew giddy. A cigar which he lighted for the purpose tranquilized him.

I hewed sixty steps upon this slope, and each step had cost a minute, by Hirst's watch. The Mur de la Côte was still before us, and on this the guide-books informed us two or three hundred steps were sometimes found necessary. If sixty steps cost an hour, what would be the cost of two hundred? The question was disheartening in the extreme, for the time at which we had calculated on reaching the summit was already passed, while the chief difficulties remained unconquered. Having hewn our way along the harder ice we reached snow. I again resorted to stamping to secure a footing, and while thus engaged became, for the first time, aware of the drain of force to which I was subjecting myself. The thought of being absolutely exhausted had never occurred to me, and from first to last I had taken no care to husband my strength. I always calculated that the "will" would serve me even should the muscles fail, but I now found that mechanical laws rule man in the long run; that no effort of will, no power of spirit, can draw beyond a certain limit upon muscular force. The soul, it is true, can stir the body to action, but its function is to excite and apply force, and not to create it.

While stamping forward through the frozen crust I was compelled to pause at short intervals; then would set out again apparently fresh, to find, however, in a few minutes, that my strength was gone, and that I required to rest once more. In this way I gained the summit

ALPINE MOUNTAIN CLIMBING

of the Corridor, when Hirst came to the front, and I felt some relief in stepping slowly after him, making use of the holes into which his feet had sunk. He thus led the way to the base of the Mur de la Côte, the thought of which had so long cast a gloom upon us; here we left our rope behind us, and while pausing I asked Simond whether he did not feel a desire to go to the summit. "Surely," was his reply, "but!——" Our guide's mind was so constituted that the "but" seemed essential to its peace. I stretched my hands toward him, and said: "Simond, we must do it." One thing alone I felt could defeat us: the usual time of the ascent had been more than doubled, the day was already far spent, and if the ascent would throw our subsequent descent into night it could not be contemplated.

We now faced the Mur, which was by no means so bad as we had expected. Driving the iron claws of our boots into the scars made by the ax, and the spikes of our batons into the slope above our feet, we ascended steadily until the summit was attained, and the top of the mountain rose clearly above us. We congratulated ourselves upon this; but Simond, probably fearing that our joy might become too full, remarked: "But the summit is still far off!" It was, alas! too true. The snow became soft again, and our weary limbs sank in it as before. Our guide went on in front, audibly muttering his doubts as to our ability to reach the top, and at length he threw himself upon the snow, and exclaimed, "I give up!"

Hirst now undertook the task of rekindling

the guide's enthusiasm, after which Simond rose, exclaiming: "Oh, but this makes my knees ache!" and went forward. Two rocks break through the snow between the summit of the Mur and the top of the mountain; the first is called the Petits Mulets, and the highest the Derniers Rochers. At the former of these we paused to rest, and finished our scanty store of wine and provisions. We had not a bit of bread nor a drop of wine left; our brandy flasks were also nearly exhausted, and thus we had to contemplate the journey to the summit, and the subsequent descent to the Grands Mulets, without the slightest prospect of physical refreshment. The almost total loss of two nights' sleep, with two days' toil superadded, made me long for a few minutes' doze, so I stretched myself upon a composite couch of snow and granite, and immediately fell asleep.

My friend, however, soon aroused me. "You quite frighten me," he said; "I have listened for some minutes, and have not heard you breathe once." I had, in reality, been taking deep draughts of the mountain air, but so silently as not to be heard.

I now filled our empty wine-bottle with snow and placed it in the sunshine, that we might have a little water on our return. We then rose; it was half-past two o'clock; we had been upward of twelve hours climbing, and I calculated that, whether we reached the summit or not, we could at all events work "toward" it for another hour. To the sense of fatigue previously experienced, a new phenomenon was now added—the beating of the heart. We were incessantly pulled up by this, which sometimes became so intense as to suggest danger. I counted the number of paces which we were able to accomplish without resting, and found that at the end of every twenty, sometimes at the end of fifteen, we were compelled to pause. At each pause my heart throbbed audibly, as I leaned upon my staff, and the subsidence of this action was always the signal for further advance. My breathing was quick, but light and unimpeded.

I endeavored to ascertain whether the hip-joint, on account of the diminished atmospheric pressure, became loosened, so as to throw the weight of the leg upon the surrounding ligaments, but could not be certain about it. I also sought a little aid and encouragement from philosophy, endeavoring to remember what great things had been done by the accumulation of small quantities, and I urged upon myself that the present was a case in point, and that the summation of distances twenty paces each must finally place us at the top. Still the question of time left the matter long in doubt, and until we had passed the Derniers Rochers we worked on with the stern indifference of men who were doing their duty, and did not look to consequences. Here, however, a gleam of hope began to brighten our souls: the summit became visible nearer, Simond showed more alacrity; at length success became certain, and at half-past three P.M. my friend and I clasped hands upon the top.

The summit of the mountain is an elongated ridge, which has been compared to the back of an ass. It was perfectly manifest that we were dominant over all other mountains; as far as the eye could range Mont Blanc had no competitor. The summits which had looked down upon us in the morning were now far beneath us. The Dôme du Gouté, which had held its threatening "séracs" above us so long, was now at our feet. The Aiguille du Midi, Mont Blanc du Tacul, and the Monts Maudits, the Talèfre, with its surrounding peaks, the Grand Jorasse, Mont Mallet, and the Aiguille du Géant, with our own familiar glaciers, were all below us. And as our eye ranged over the broad shoulders of the mountain, over ice hills and valleys, plateaux and far-stretching slopes of snow, the conception of its magnitude grew upon us, and imprest us more and more.

The clouds were very grand—grander, indeed, than anything I had ever before seen. Some of them seemed to hold thunder in their breasts, they were so dense and dark; others, with their faces turned sunward, shone with the dazzling whiteness of the mountain snow; while others again built themselves into forms resembling gigantic elm trees, loaded with foliage. Toward the horizon the luxury of color added itself to the magnificent alternation of light and shade. Clear spaces of amber and ethereal green embraced the red and purple cumuli, and seemed to form the cradle in which they swung. Closer at hand squally mists, suddenly engendered, were driven hither and thither by local winds; while the clouds at a distance lay "like angels sleeping on the wing," with scarcely visibly motion. Mingling with the clouds, and sometimes rising above them, were the highest mountain heads, and as our eyes wandered from peak to peak, onward to the remote horizon, space itself seemed more vast from the manner in which the objects which it held were distributed. . . .

The day was waning, and, urged by the warnings of our ever-prudent guide, we at length began the descent. Gravity was in our favor, but gravity could not entirely spare our wearied limbs, and where we sank in the snow we found our downward progress very trying. I suffered from thirst, but after we had divided the liquefied snow at the Petits Mulets among us we had nothing to drink. I crammed the clean snow into my mouth, but the process of melting was slow and tantalizing to a parched throat, while the chill was painful to the teeth.

THE JUNGFRAU-JOCH*

BY SIR LESLIE STEPHEN

I was once more standing upon the Wengern Alp, and gazing longingly at the Jungfrau-Joch. Surely the Wengern Alp must be precisely the lovliest place in this world. To hurry past it, and listen to the roar of the avalanches, is a very unsatisfactory mode of enjoyment; it reminds one too much of letting off crackers in a cathedral. The mountains seem to be accomplices of the people who charge fifty centimes for an echo. But it does one's moral nature good to linger there at sunset or in the early morning, when tourists have

*From "The Playground of Europe." Published by Longmans, Green & Co.

ceased from traveling; and the jaded cockney may enjoy a kind of spiritual bath in the soothing calmness of scenery. . . .

We, that is a little party of six Englishmen with six Oberland guides, who left the inn at 3 A.M. on July 20, 1862, were not, perhaps, in a specially poetical mood. Yet as the sun rose while we were climbing the huge buttress of the Mönch, the dullest of us—I refer, of course, to myself—felt something of the spirit of the scenery. The day was cloudless, and a vast inverted cone of dazzling rays suddenly struck upward into the sky through the gap between the Mönch and the Eiger, which, as some effect of perspective shifted its apparent position, looked like a glory streaming from the very summit of the Eiger. It was a good omen, if not in any more remote sense, yet as promising a fine day. After a short climb we descended upon the Gugg, glacier, most lamentably unpoetical of names, and mounted by it to the great plateau which lies below the cliffs immediately under the col. We reached this at about seven, and, after a short meal, carefully examined the route above us. Half way between us and the col lay a small and apparently level plateau of snow. Once upon it we felt confident that we could get to the top. . . .

We plunged at once into the maze of crevasses, finding our passage much facilitated by the previous efforts of our guides. We were constantly walking over ground strewed with crumbling blocks of ice, the recent fall of which was proved by their sharp white fractures, and with a thing like an infirm toad stool twenty feet high, towering above our heads. Once we passed under a

ALPINE MOUNTAIN CLIMBING

natural arch of ice, built in evident disregard of all principles of architectural stability. Hurrying judiciously at such critical points, and creeping slowly round those where the footing was difficult, we manage to thread the labyrinth safely, whilst Rubi appeared to think it rather pleasant than otherwise in such places to have his head fixt in a kind of pillory between two rungs of a ladder, with twelve feet of it sticking out behind and twelve feet before him.

We reached the gigantic crevasse at 7.35. We passed along it to a point where its two lips nearly joined, and the side furthest from us was considerably higher than that upon which we stood. Fixing the foot of the ladder upon this ledge, we swung the top over, and found that it rested satisfactorily against the opposite bank. Almer crept up it, and made the top firmer by driving his ax into the snow underneath the highest step. The rest of us followed, carefully roped, and with the caution to rest our knees on the sides of the ladder, as several of the steps were extremely weak —a remark which was equally applicable to one, at least, of the sides. We crept up the rickety old machine, however, looking down between our legs into the blue depths of the crevasse, and at 8.15 the whole party found itself satisfactorily perched on the edge of the nearly level snow plateau, looking up at the long slopes of broken névé that led to the col. . . .

When the man behind was also engaged in hauling himself up by the rope attached to your waist, when the two portions of the rope formed an acute angle, when your footing was confined to the insecure grip of one toe on a slippery bit of ice, and when a great hummock of hard sérac was pressing against the pit of your stomach and reducing you to a position of neutral equilibrium, the result was a feeling of qualified acquiescence in Michel or Almer's lively suggestion of "Vorwärts! vorwärts!"

Somehow or other we did ascend. The excitement made the time seem short; and after what seemed to me to be half an hour, which was in fact nearly two hours, we had crept, crawled, climbed and wormed our way through various obstacles, till we found ourselves brought up by a huge overhanging wall of blue ice. This wall was no doubt the upper side of a crevasse, the lower part of which had been filled by snow-drift. Its face was honeycombed by the usual hemispherical chippings, which somehow always reminds me of the fretted walls of the Alhambra; and it was actually hollowed out so that its upper edge overhung our heads at a height of some twenty or thirty feet; the long fringe of icicles which adorned it had made a slippery pathway of ice at two or three feet distance from the foot of the wall by the freezing water which dripped from them; and along this we crept, in hopes that none of the icicles would come down bodily.

The wall seemed to thin out and become much lower toward our left, and we moved cautiously toward its lowest point. The edge upon which we walked was itself very narrow, and ran down at a steep angle to the top of a lower icefall which repeated the form of the upper. It almost thinned out at the point where the upper wall was lowest. Upon this inclined ledge, however, we fixt the foot of our ladder. The difficulty of do-

ALPINE MOUNTAIN CLIMBING

ing so conveniently was increased by a transverse crevasse which here intersected the other system. The foot, however, was fixt and rendered tolerably safe by driving in firmly several of our alpenstocks and axes under the lowest step. Almer, then, amidst great excitement, went forward to mount it. Should we still find an impassable system of crevasses above us, or were we close to the top? A gentle breeze which had been playing along the last ledge gave me hope that we were really not far off. As Almer reached the top about twelve o'clock, a loud yodel gave notice to all the party that our prospects were good. I soon followed, and saw, to my great delight, a stretch of smooth, white snow, without a single crevasse, rising in a gentle curve from our feet to the top of the col.

The people who had been watching us from the Wengern Alp had been firing salutes all day, whenever the idea struck them, and whenever we surmounted a difficulty, such as the first great crevasse. We heard the faint sound of two or three guns as we reached the final plateau. We should, properly speaking, have been uproariously triumphant over our victory. To say the truth, our party of that summer was only too apt to break out into undignified explosions of animal spirits, bordering at times upon horseplay. . . .

The top of the Jungfrau-Joch comes rather like a bathos in poetry. It rises so gently above the steep ice wall, and it is so difficult to determine the precise culminating point, that our enthusiasm oozed out gradually instead of producing a sudden explosion; and that instead of giving three cheers, singing "God Save the Queen," or observ-

SEEING EUROPE WITH FAMOUS AUTHORS

ing any of the traditional ceremonial of a simpler generation of travelers, we calmly walked forward as tho we had been crossing Westminster Bridge, and on catching sight of a small patch of rocks near the foot of the Mönch, rushed precipitately down to it and partook of our third breakfast. Which things, like most others, might easily be made into an allegory.

The great dramatic moments of life are very apt to fall singularly flat. We manage to discount all their interest beforehand; and are amazed to find that the day to which we have looked forward so long—the day, it may be, of our marriage, or ordination, or election to be Lord Mayor—finds us curiously unconscious of any sudden transformation and as strongly inclined to prosaic eating and drinking as usual. At a later period we may become conscious of its true significance, and perhaps the satisfactory conquest of this new pass has given us more pleasure in later years than it did at the moment.

However that may be, we got under way again after a meal and a chat, our friends Messrs. George and Moore descending the Aletsch glacier to the Aeggischhorn, whose summit was already in sight, and deceptively near in appearance. The remainder of the party soon turned off to the left, and ascended the snow slopes to the gap between the Mönch and Trugberg. As we passed these huge masses, rising in solitary grandeur from the center of one of the noblest snowy wastes of the Alps, Morgan reluctantly confest for the first time that he knew nothing exactly like it in Wales.

XI

OTHER ALPINE TOPICS

THE GREAT ST. BERNARD HOSPICE*

BY ARCHIBALD CAMPBELL KNOWLES

The Pass of the Great St. Bernard was a well-known one long before the hospice was built. Before the Christian era, the Romans used it as a highway across the Alps, constantly improving the road as travel over it increased. Many lives were lost, however, as no material safeguards could obviate the danger from the elements, and no one will ever know the number of souls who met their end in the blinding snows and chilling blasts of those Alpine heights.

To Bernard de Menthon is due the credit of the mountain hospice. He was the originator of the idea and the founder of the institution. He has since been canonized as a saint and he well deserved the honor, if it be a virtue to sacrifice oneself, as we believe, and to try and save the lives of one's fellows! It is no easy existence which St. Bernard chose for himself and followers. The very aspect of the pass is grand but gloomy. None of the softness of nature is seen. There is no ver-

*From "Adventures in the Alps." Published by the George W. Jacob Co.

SEEING EUROPE WITH FAMOUS AUTHORS

dure, no beauty of coloring, nothing but bleak, bare rock, great piles of stones, and occasional patches of fallen snow. It is thoroughly exposed, the winds always moaning mournfully around the buildings. . . .

The trip begins at Martigny. First there is a level stretch, then a long, steady climb, after which begins the real road to the pass. The views are very lovely, and while quite different in some ways excel all passes except the famous Simplon. The scenery is very varied, the mountains are far enough off to give a good perspective, and the villages are most picturesque. The absence of snow peaks in any great number will be felt by some, but even a lover of such soon forgets the lack in the exceeding beauty and loveliness of the valleys.

Toward the top of the pass there is quite a transformation. Both the road and the scenery change, the first becoming more and more steep and stony, the latter showing more and more of savage grandeur, as the green, smiling valleys are no longer seen, but in their place appear barren and rugged rocks and slopes, with the marks of the ravages wrought by storm, landslide and avalanche. The wind has fuller play and seems to moan in a mournful, dirge-like manner, accentuating the characteristics of bleakness and desolation which obtain at the top of the pass, all the more noticeable if the traveler arrives at dusk, just as the sun has disappeared behind the mountains.

In this dreary place stands the hospice. The present buildings are not very old, the hospice only dating from the sixteenth century and the

OTHER ALPINE TOPICS

church from the seventeenth century, while the other structures, which have been built for the accommodation of strangers are comparatively new. Twelve monks of the Augustinian Order are regularly in residence here. They come when about twenty years of age; but so severe is the climate, so hard the life and so stern the rule that, after a service of about fifteen years, they generally have to seek a lower altitude, often ruined in health, with their powers completely sapped by the rigors and privations which they have endured. Altho the hospice and the adjoining hostelry for the travelers are cheerless in the extreme, there is always a warm welcome from the monks. No one, however poor, is refused bed and board for the night, and there is no "distinction of persons." The hospitality is extended to all, free of charge, this being the invariable rule of the institution, but it is expected, and rightly so, that those who can do so will deposit a liberal offering in the box provided for the purpose. The small receipts, however, show what a great abuse there is of this hospitality, for a large number of those who come in the summer could well afford to give and to give largely.

We hear much of the courage and perseverance of Hannibal and Cæsar in leading their armies over the Alps! We see pictures of Napoleon and his soldiers as they toiled up the pass, dragging along their frozen guns, and perhaps falling into a fatal sleep about their dying camp fires at night! And we rightly admire such bravery, and thrill with admiration at the tale. Yet those armies which crossed the Alps failed to equal the heroic self-sacrifice of those soldiers of the cross, the

Monks of the Grand St. Bernard, who remain for years at their post, unknown and unsung by the wide, wide world, simply to save and shelter the humble travelers who come to grief in their winter journey across the pass, in search of work.

AVALANCHES*

BY VICTOR TISSOT

Beside this dazzling, magnificent snow, covering the chain of lofty peaks like an immaculate altar cloth, what a gloomy, dull look there is in the snow of the plains! One might think it was made of sugar or confectionery, that it was false like all the rest.

To know what snow really is—to get quit of this feeling of artificial snow that we have when we see the stunted shrubs in our Parisian gardens wrapt, as it were, in silk paper like bits of Christmas trees—it must be seen here in these far-off, high valleys of the Engandine, that lie for eight months dead under their shroud of snow, and often, even in the height of summer, have to shiver anew under some wintry flakes.

It is here that snow is truly beautiful! It shines in the sun with a dazzling whiteness; it sparkles with a thousand fires like diamond dust; it shows gleams like the plumage of a white dove, and it is as firm under the foot as a marble pavement. It is so fine-grained, so

*From "Unknown Switzerland." Published by James Pott & Co.

OTHER ALPINE TOPICS

compact, that it clings like dust to every crevice and bend, to every projecting edge and point, and follows every outline of the mountain, the form of which it leaves as clearly delined as if it were a covering of thin gauze. It sports in the most charming decorations, carves alabaster facings and cornices on the cliffs, wreathes them in delicate lace, covers them with vast canopies of white satin spangled with stars and fringed with silver.

And yet this dry, hard snow is extremely susceptible to the slightest shock, and may be set in motion by a very trifling disturbance of the air. The flight of a bird, the cracking of a whip, the tinkling of bells, even the conversation of persons going along sometimes suffices to shake and loosen it from the vertical face of the cliffs to which it is clinging; and it runs down like grains of sand, growing as it falls, by drawing down with it other beds of snow. It is like a torrent, a snowy waterfall, bursting out suddenly from the side of the mountain; it rushes down with a terrible noise, swollen with the snows that it carries down in its furious course; it breaks against the rocks, divides and joins again like an overflowing stream, and with a wild tempest blast resumes its desolating course, filling the echoes with the deafening thunder of battle.

You think for a moment that a storm has begun, but looking at the sky you see it serenely blue, smiling, cloudless. The rush becomes more and more violent; it comes nearer, the ground trembles, the trees bend and break with a sharp crack; enormous stones and blocks of ice are carried away like gravel; and the mighty avalanche, with a crash like a train running off the rails over a precipice, drops to the foot of the mountain, destroying, crushing down everything before it, and covering the ground with a bed of snow from thirty to fifty feet deep.

When a stream of water wears a passage for itself under this compact mass, it is sometimes hollowed out into an arched way, and the snow becomes so solid that carriages and horses can go through without danger, even in the middle of summer. But often the water does not find a course by which to flow away; and then, when the snow begins to melt, the water seeps into the fissures, loosens the mass that chokes up the valley, and carries it down, rending its banks as it goes, carrying away bridges, mills, and trees, and overthrowing houses. The avalanche has become an inundation.

The mountaineers make a distinction between summer and winter avalanches. The former are solid avalanches, formed of old snow that has almost acquired the consistency of ice. The warm breath of spring softens it, loosens it from the rocks on which it hangs, and it slides down into the valleys. These are called "melting avalanches." They regularly follow certain tracks, and these are embanked, like the course of a river, with wood or bundles of branches. It is in order to protect the alpine roads from these avalanches that those long open galleries have been built on the face of the precipice.

The most dreaded and most terrible avalanches, those of dry, powdery snow, occur only

OTHER ALPINE TOPICS

in winter, when sudden squalls and hurricanes of snow throw the whole atmosphere into chaos. They come down in sudden whirlwinds, with the violence of a waterspout, and in a few minutes whole villages are buried. . . .

Here, in the Grisons, the whole village of Selva was buried under an avalanche. Nothing remained visible but the top of the church steeple, looking like a pole planted in the snow. Baron Munchausen might have tied his horse there without inventing any lie about it. The Val Verzasca was covered for several months by an avalanche of nearly 1,000 feet in length and 50 in depth. All communication through the valley was stopt; it was impossible to organize help; and the alarm-bell was incessantly sounding over the immense white desolation like a knell for the dead.

In the narrow defile in which we now are, there are many remains of avalanches that neither the water of the torrent nor the heat of the sun has had power to melt. The bed of the river is strewn with displaced and broken rocks, and great stones bound together by the snow as if with cement; the surges dash against these rocky obstacles, foaming angrily, with the blind fury of a wild beast. And the moan of the powerless water flows on into the depth of the valley, and is lost far off in a hollow murmur.

HUNTING THE CHAMOIS*

BY VICTOR TISSOT

Schmidt swept with his cap the snow which covered the stones on which we were to seat ourselves for breakfast, then unpacked the provisions; slices of veal and ham, hard-boiled eggs, wine of the Valtelline. His knapsack, covered with a napkin, served for our table. While we sat, we devoured the landscape, the twelve glaciers spreading around us their carpet of swansdown and ermine, sinking into crevasses of a magical transparency, and raising their blocks, shaped into needles, or into Gothic steeples with pierced arches. The architecture of the glacier is marvelous. Its decorations are the decorations of fairyland. Quite near us marks of animals in the snow attracted our attention. Schmidt said to us:

"Chamois have been here this morning; the traces are quite fresh. They must have seen us and made off; the chamois are as distrustful, you see, as the marmots, and as wary. At this season they keep on the glaciers by preference. They live on so little! A few herbs, a few mosses, such as grow on isolated rocks like this. I assure you it is very amusing to see a herd of twenty or thirty chamois cross at a headlong pace a vast field of snow, or glacier, where they bound over the crevasses in play.

"One would say they were reindeers in a Lapland scene. It is only at night that they

*From "Unknown Switzerland." Published by James Pott & Co.

178

OTHER ALPINE TOPICS

come down into the valleys. In the moonlight they come out of the moraines, and go to pasture on the grassy slopes or in the forest adjoining the glaciers. During the day they go up again into the snow, for which they have an extraordinary love, and in which they skip and play, amusing themselves like a band of scholars in play hours. They tease one another, butt with their horns in fun, run off, return, pretend new attacks and new flights with charming agility and frolicsomeness.

"While the young ones give themselves up to their sports, an old female, posted as sentinel at some yards distance, watches the valley and scents the air. At the slightest indication of danger, she utters a sharp cry; the games cease instantly, and the whole anxious troop assembles round the guardian, then the whole herd sets off at a gallop and disappears in the twinkling of an eye. . . .

"Hunting on the névés and the glaciers is very dangerous. When the snow is fresh it is with difficulty one can advance. The hunters use wooden snowshoes, like those of the Esquimaux.

"One of my comrades, in hunting on the Roseg, disappeared in the bottom of a crevasse. It was over thirty feet deep. Imagine two perfectly smooth sides; two walls of crystal. To reascend was impossible. It was certain death, either from cold or hunger; for it was known that when he went chamois-hunting he was often absent for several days. He could not therefore count on help being sent; he must resign himself to death.

"One thing, however, astonished him; it was to find so little water in the bottom of the crevasse. Could there be then an opening at the bottom of the funnel into which he had fallen? He stooped, examined this grave in which he had been buried alive, discovered that the heat of the sun had caused the base of the glacier to melt. A canal drainage had been formed. Laying himself flat, he slid into this dark passage, and after a thousand efforts he arrived at the end of the glacier in the moraine, safe and sound."

We had finished breakfast. We wanted something warm, a little coffee. Schmidt set up our spirit-lamp behind two great stones that protected it from the wind. And while we waited for the water to boil, he related to us the story of Colani, the legendary hunter of the upper Engandine.

"Colani, in forty years, killed two thousand seven hundred chamois. This strange man had carved out for himself a little kingdom in the mountain. He claimed to reign there alone, to be absolute master. When a stranger penetrated into his residence, within the domain of 'his reserved hunting-ground,' as he called the regions of the Bernina, he treated him as a poacher, and chased him with a gun. . . .

"Colani was feared and dreaded as a diabolical and supernatural being; and indeed he took no pains to undeceive the public, for the superstitious terrors inspired by his person served to keep away all the chamois-hunters from his chamois, which he cared for and managed as a great lord cares for the deer in his forests.

Round the little house which he had built for himself on the Col de Bernina, and where he passed the summer and autumn, two hundred chamois, almost tame, might be seen wandering about and browsing. Every year he killed about fifty old males."

THE CELEBRITIES OF GENEVA*

BY FRANCIS H. GRIBBLE

It has been remarked as curious that the Age of Revolution at Geneva was also the Golden Age —if not of Genevan literature, which has never really had any Golden Age, at least of Genevan science, which was of world-wide renown.

The period is one in which notable names meet us at every turn. There were exiled Genevans, like de Lolme, holding their own in foreign political and intellectual circles; there were emigrant Genevan pastors holding aloft the lamps of culture and piety in many cities of England, France, Russia, Germany, and Denmark; there were Genevans, like François Lefort, holding the highest offices in the service of foreign rulers; and there were numbers of Genevans at Geneva of whom the cultivated grand tourist wrote in the tone of a disciple writing of his master. One can not glance at the history of the period without lighting upon names of note in almost all departments of endeavor. The period is that of de Saussure, Bourrit, the de Lucs, the two Hubers, great authorities respectively on bees and birds; Le

*From "Geneva."

Sage, who was one of Gibbon's rivals for the heart of Mademoiselle Suzanne Curchod; Senebier, the librarian who wrote the first literary history of Geneva; St. Ours and Arlaud, the painters; Charles Bonnet, the entomologist; Bérenger and Picot, the historians; Tronchin, the physician; Trembley and Jallabert, the mathematicians; Dentan, minister and Alpine explorer; Pictet, the editor of the "Bibliothèque Universelle," still the leading Swiss literary review; and Odier, who taught Geneva the virtue of vaccination.

It is obviously impossible to dwell at length upon the careers of all these eminent men. As well might one attempt, in a survey on the same scale of English literature, to discuss in detail the careers of all the celebrities of the age of Anne. One can do little more than remark that the list is marvelously strong for a town of some 30,000 inhabitants, and that many of the names included in it are not only eminent, but interesting. Jean André de Luc, for example, has a double claim upon our attention as the inventor of the hygrometer and as the pioneer of the snow-peaks. He climbed the Buet as early as 1770, and wrote an account of his adventures on its summit and its slopes which has the true charm of Arcadian simplicity. He came to England, was appointed reader to Queen Charlotte, and lived in the enjoyment of that office, and in the gratifying knowledge that Her Majesty kept his presentation hygrometer in her private apartments, to the venerable age of ninety.

Bourrit is another interesting character—being, in fact, the spiritual ancestor of the modern Alpine Clubman. By profession he was Precentor

OTHER ALPINE TOPICS

of the Cathedral; but his heart was in the mountains. In the summer he climbed them, and in the winter he wrote books about them. One of his books was translated into English; and the list of subscribers, published with the translation, shows that the public which Bourrit addrest included Edmund Burke, Sir Joseph Banks, Bartolozzi, Fanny Burney, Angelica Kauffman, David Garrick, Sir Joshua Reynolds, George Augustus Selwyn, Jonas Hanway and Dr. Johnson. His writings earned him the honorable title of Historian (or Historiographer) of the Alps. Men of science wrote him letters; princes engaged upon the grand tour called to see him; princesses sent him presents as tokens of their admiration and regard for the man who had taught them how the contemplation of mountain scenery might exalt the sentiments of the human mind.

Tronchin, too, is interesting; he was the first physician who recognized the therapeutic use of fresh air and exercise, hygienic boots, and open windows. So is Charle Bonnet, who was not afraid to stand up for orthodoxy against Voltaire; so is Mallet, who traveled as far as Lapland; and so is that man of whom his contemporaries always spoke, with the reverence of hero-worshipers, as "the illustrious de Saussure." . . .

The name of which the Genevans are proudest is probably that of Rousseau, who has sometimes been spoken of as "the austere citizen of Geneva." But "austere" is a strange epithet to apply to the philosopher who endowed the Foundling Hospital with five illegitimate children; and Geneva can not claim a great share in a citizen who ran away from the town of his boyhood to avoid being thrashed for stealing apples. It was, indeed, at Geneva that Jean Jacques received from his aunt the disciplinary chastisement of which he gives such an exciting account in his "Confessions"; and he once returned to the city and received the Holy Communion there in later life. But that is all. Jean Jacques was not educated at Geneva, but in Savoy—at Annecy, at Turin, and at Chambéry; his books were not printed at Geneva, tho one of them was publicly burned there, but in Paris and Amsterdam; it is not to Genevan but to French literature that he belongs.

We must visit Voltaire at Ferney, and Madame de Staël at Coppet. Let the patriarch come first. Voltaire was sixty years of age when he settled on the shores of the lake, where he was to remain for another four-and-twenty years; and he did not go there for his pleasure. He would have preferred to live in Paris, but was afraid of being locked up in the Bastille. As the great majority of the men of letters of the reign of Louis XV. were, at one time or another, locked up in the Bastille, his fears were probably well founded.

Moreover, notes of warning had reached his ears. "I dare not ask you to dine," a relative said to him, "because you are in bad odor at Court." So he betook himself to Geneva, as so many Frenchmen, illustrious and otherwise, had done before, and acquired various properties—at Prangins, at Lausanne, at Saint-Jean (near Geneva), at Ferney, at Tournay, and elsewhere.

He was welcomed cordially. Dr. Tronchin, the eminent physician, cooperated in the legal fictions necessary to enable him to become a landowner in the republic. Cramer, the publisher, made a

OTHER ALPINE TOPICS

proposal for the issue of a complete and authorized edition of his works. All the best people called. "It is very pleasant," he was able to write, "to live in a country where rulers borrow your carriage to come to dinner with you."

Voltaire corresponded regularly with at least four reigning sovereigns, to say nothing of men of letters, Cardinals, and Marshals of France; and he kept open house for travelers of mark from every country in the world. Those of the travelers who wrote books never failed to devote a chapter to an account of a visit to Ferney; and from the mass of such descriptions we may select for quotation that written, in the stately style of the period, by Dr. John Moore, author of "Zeluco," then making the grand tour as tutor to the Duke of Hamilton.

"The most piercing eyes I ever beheld," the doctor writes, "are those of Voltaire, now in his eightieth year. His whole countenance is expressive of genius, observation, and extreme sensibility. In the morning he has a look of anxiety and discontent; but this gradually wears off, and after dinner he seems cheerful; yet an air of irony never entirely forsakes his face, but may always be observed lurking in his features whether he frowns or smiles. Composition is his principal amusement. No author who writes for daily bread, no young poet ardent for distinction, is more assiduous with his pen, or more anxious for fresh fame, than the wealthy and applauded Seigneur of Ferney. He lives in a very hospitable manner, and takes care always to have a good cook. He generally has two or three visitors from Paris, who stay with him a month or six weeks at a time. When they go, their places are soon supplied, so that there is a constant rotation of society at Ferney. These, with Voltaire's own family and his visitors from Geneva, compose a company of twelve or fourteen people, who dine daily at his table, whethers he appears or not. All who bring recommendations from his friends may depend upon being received, if he be not really indisposed. He often presents himself to the strangers who assemble every afternoon in his antechamber, altho they bring no particular recommendation."

It might have been added that (when an interesting stranger who carried no introduction was passing through the town, Voltaire sometimes sent for him; but this experiment was not always a success, and failed most ludicrously in the case of Claude Gay, the Philadelphian Quaker, author of some theological works now forgotten, but then of note. The meeting was only arranged with difficulty on the philosopher's undertaking to put a bridle on his tongue, and say nothing flippant about holy things. He tried to keep his promise, but the temptation was too strong for him. After a while he entangled his guest in a controversy concerning the proceedings of the patriarchs and the evidences of Christianity, and lost his temper on finding that his sarcasms failed to make their usual impression. The member of the Society of Friends, however, was not disconcerted. He rose from his place at the dinner-table, and replied: "Friend Voltaire! perhaps thou mayst come to understand these matters rightly; in the meantime, finding I can do thee no good, I leave thee, and so fare thee well."

OTHER ALPINE TOPICS

And so saying, he walked out and walked back to Geneva, while Voltaire retired in dudgeon to his room, and the company sat expecting something terrible to happen.

A word, in conclusion, about Coppet!

Necker* bought the property from his old banking partner, Thelusson, for 500,000 livres in French money, and retired to live there when the French Revolution drove him out of politics. His daughter, Madame de Staël, inherited it from him, and made it famous.

Not that she loved Switzerland; it would be more true to say that she detested Switzerland. Swiss scenery meant nothing to her. When she was taken for an excursion to the glaciers, she asked what the crime was that she had to expiate by such a punishment; and she could look out on the blue waters of Lake Leman, and sigh for "the gutter of the Rue du Bac." Even to this day, the Swiss have hardly forgiven her for that, or for speaking of the Canton of Vaud as the country in which she had been "so intensely bored for such a number of years."

What she wanted was to live in Paris, to be a leader—or, rather, to be "the" leader—of Parisian society, to sit in a salon, the admired of all admirers, and to pull the wires of politics to the advantage of her friends. For a while she succeeded in doing this. It was she who persuaded Barras to give Talleyrand his political start in life. But whereas Barras was willing to act on her advice, Napoleon was by no means equally amenable to her influence. Almost from

*The French financier and minister of Louis XVI., father of Madame de Staël.

the first he regarded her as a mischief-maker; and when a spy brought him an intercepted letter in which Madame de Staël expressed her hope that none of the old aristocracy of France would condescend to accept appointments in the household of "the bourgeois of Corsica," he became her personal enemy, and, refusing her permission to live either in the capital or near it, practically compelled her to take refuge in her country seat. Her pleasaunce in that way became her gilded cage.

Perhaps she was not quite so unhappy there as she sometimes represented. If she could not go to Paris, many distinguished and brilliant Parisians came to Coppet, and met there many brilliant and distinguished Germans, Genevans, Italians, and Danes. The Parisian salon, reconstituted, flourished on Swiss soil. There visited there, at one time or another, Madame Récamier and Madame Krüdner; Benjamin Constant, who was so long Madame de Staël's lover; Bonstetten, the Voltairean philosopher; Frederika Brun, the Danish artist; Sismondi, the historian; Werner, the German poet; Karl Ritter, the German geographer; Baron de Voght; Monti, the Italian poet: Madame Vigée Le Brun; Cuvier; and Oelenschlaeger. From almost every one of them we have some pen-and-ink sketch of the life there. This, for instance, is the scene as it appeared to Madame Le Brun, who came to paint the hostess's portrait:

"I paint her in antique costume. She is not beautiful, but the animation of her visage takes the place of beauty. To aid the expression I wished to give her, I entreated her to recite tragic verses while I painted. She declaimed passages from

OTHER ALPINE TOPICS

Corneille and Racine. I find many persons established at Coppet. the beautiful Madame Récamier, the Comte de Sabran, a young English woman, Benjamin Constant, etc. Its society is continually renewed. They come to visit the illustrious exile who is pursued by the rancor of the Emperor. Her two sons are now with her, under the instruction of the German scholar Schlegel; her daughter is very beautiful, and has a passionate love of study; she leaves her company free all the morning, but they unite in the evening. It is only after dinner that they can converse with her. She then walks in her salon, holding in her hand a little green branch; and her words have an ardor quite peculiar to her; it is impossible to interrupt her. At these times she produces on one the effect of an improvisatrice."

And here is a still more graphic description, taken from a letter written to Madame Récamier by Baron de Voght:

"It is to you that I owe my most amiable reception at Coppet. It is no doubt to the favorable expectations aroused by your friendship that I owe my intimate acquaintance with this remarkable woman. I might have met her without your assistance—some casual acquaintance would no doubt have introduced me—but I should never have penetrated to the intimacy of this sublime and beautiful soul, and should never have known how much better she is than her reputation. She is an angel sent from heaven to reveal the divine goodness upon earth. To make her irresistible, a pure ray of celestial light embellishes her spirit and makes her amiable from every point of view.

"At once profound and light, whether she is

discovering a mysterious secret of the soul or grasping the lightest shadow of a sentiment, her genius shines without dazzling, and when the orb of light has disappeared, it leaves a pleasant twilight to follow it. . . . No doubt a few faults, a few weaknesses, occasionally veil this celestial apparition; even the initiated must sometimes be troubled by these eclipses, which the Genevan astronomers in vain endeavor to predict.

"My travels so far have been limited to journeys to Lausanne and Coppet, where I often stay three or four days. The life there suits me perfectly; the company is even more to my taste. I like Constant's wit, Schlegel's learning, Sabran's amiability, Sismondi's talent and character, the simple truthful disposition and just intellectual perceptions of Auguste,* the wit and sweetness of Albertine†—I was forgetting Bonstetten, an excellent fellow, full of knowledge of all sorts, ready in wit, adaptable in character—in every way inspiring one's respect and confidence.

"Your sublime friend looks and gives life to everything. She imparts intelligence to those around her. In every corner of the house some one is engaged in composing a great work. . . . Corinne is writing her delightful letters about Germany, which will, no doubt, prove to be the best thing she has ever done.

"The 'Shunamitish Widow,' an Oriental melodrama which she has just finished, will be played

*Madame de Staël's son, who afterward edited the works of Madame de Staël and Madame Necker.—Author's note.

†Madame de Staël's daughter, afterward Duchesse de Broglie.

OTHER ALPINE TOPICS

in October; it is charming. Coppet will be flooded with tears. Constant and Auguste are both composing tragedies; Sabran is writing a comic opera, and Sismondi a history; Schlegel is translating something; Bonstetten is busy with philosophy, and I am busy with my letter to Juliette."

Then, a month later:

"Since my last letter, Madame de Staël has read us several chapters of her work. Everywhere it bears the marks of her talent. I wish I could persuade her to cut out everything in it connected with politics, and all the metaphors which interfere with its clarity, simplicity, and accuracy. What she needs to demonstrate is not he republicanism, but her wisdom. Mlle. Jenner played in one of Werner's tragedies which was given, last Friday, before an audience of twenty. She, Werner, and Schlegel played perfectly. . . .

"The arrival in Switzerland of M. Cuvier has been a happy distraction for Madame de Staël; they spent two days together at Geneva, and were well pleased with each other. On her return to Coppet she found Middleton there, and in receiving his confidences forgot her troubles. Yesterday she resumed her work.

"The poet whose mystical and somber genius has caused us such profound emotions starts, in a few days' time, for Italy.

"I accompanied Corinne to Massot's. To alleviate the tedium of the sitting, a Mlle. Romilly played pleasantly on the harp, and the studio was a veritable temple of the Muses. . . .

"Bonstetten gave us two readings of a Memoir on the Northern Alps. It began very well, but afterward it bored us. Madame de Staël resumed her reading, and there was no longer any question of being bored. It is marvelous how much she must have read and thought over to be able to find the opportunity of saying so many good things. One may differ from her, but one can not help delighting in her talent. . . .

"And now here we are at Geneva, trying to reproduce Coppet at the Hôtel des Balances. I am delightfully situated with a wide view over the Valley of Savoy, between the Alps and the Jura.

Yesterday evening the illusion of Coppet was complete. I had been with Madame de Staël to call on Madame Rilliet, who is so charming at her own fireside. On my return I played chess with Sismondi. Madame de Staël, Mlle. Randall, and Mlle. Jenner sat on the sofa chatting with Bonstetten and young Barante. We were as we had always been—as we were in the days that I shall never cease regretting."

Other descriptions exist in great abundance, but these suffice to serve our purpose. They show us the Coppet salon as it was pleasant, brilliant, unconventional; something like Holland House, but more Bohemian; something like Harley Street, but more select; something like Gad's Hill—which it resembled in the fact that the members of the house-parties were expected to spend their mornings at their desks—but on a higher social plane; a center at once of high thinking and frivolous behavior; of hard work and desperate love-making, which sometimes paved the way to trouble.